How this works.....................................

"Well, here we go again. ... Did anyone here not eat his or her homework on the way to school?"

HAVE THIS WORKBOOK IN FRONT OF YOU DURING EVERY CLASS SESSION

Use for:

Review Questions: Each week has a set of review questions that covers three areas:

> 1. Material taught in class. You'll be answering these during class.
> 2. Activity questions from the previous weeks' activity
> 3. Your textbook reading assignment.

Answer all the questions in this workbook first; then before the week is out, log into PSL and transcribe the answers.

Weekly Activities: These are homework assignments also in PSL. Sometimes you'll be scanning or taking a picture of these pages to put in the drop box.

Weeks 11, 13 & 14 reading assignments: Three chapters from Edward Maunder's book "Astronomy and the Bible."

Class Schedule, Project and Grading

Week	Classroom Topics	Textbook Topics	Activities
1	**Prehistoric & Classical**	*Prologue*	**Backyard Compass**
2	**Renaissance**	**Ch 1:** *The Light He Called Day*	**Backyard Compass & Ellipse**
3	**Enlightenment & Modern**	**Ch 2:** *The Darkness He Called Night*	**Polaris and Circumpolar Stars**
4*	**The Earth**	**Ch 3:** *The Cycle of the Month*	**Azimuth and Elevation Part I**
5	**The Moon**	**Ch 4:** *The Tabernacle for the Sun*	**Tides**
6	**The Sun**	**Ch 5:** *The Cycle of the Year*	**Autumn Equinox**
7*	**Terrestrial Planets**	**Ch 6:** *The Seasonal Skies*	**Moon**
8	**The Outer Planets**	**Ch 7:** *The Wandering Stars*	**Milky Way**
9	**Dwarf Planets, Comets, Asteroids etc**	**Farmer's Almanac**	**Zodiac and Meteors**
10*	**The Milky Way Galaxy**	**Farmer's Almanac**	**Winter Zodiac & Algol**
11	**What lies Beyond**	**Maunder: Ch 1**	**Spring Zodiac & Planets**
12	**History of the Calendar and Easter**	**Epilogue:** *The Calendar*	**Azimuth and Elevation Part II**
13	**The Bible and the Constellations Part I**	**Maunder: Ch 2**	**Winter Items**
14*	**The Bible and the Constellations Part II**	**Maunder: Ch 3**	**Catch up on missed lab assignments**
15	**The Star of Bethlehem**		**Astronomy Club Visit due** [1]

* Section Exams

Class Project: Make contact with an Astronomy Club in your area; then go visit one of their evening star gazing events. Write a one-page paper describing your experience; who did you find? How did you find them? Where did you go? When did you go? What did you see and learn that evening? How did you like the experience? The paper is due any time before the last week of class.

Weekly Review Questions ....30% of final grade
Activities ....20% of final grade
Section Exams .... 20% of final grade
Astronomy Club Visit & Report ....10% of final grade
Final Exam ....20% of final grade

Week 1 Review Questions

From Class

1. According to Lt Col D. who knows more about movement of celestial bodies, the constellations and the phases of the moon?

    a. A typical public high school student   b. Home-schooled students

    c. Teenagers before our modern times   d. Democrats

2. Where is our solar system's asteroid belt?

    a. Between Earth and Mars   b. It doesn't have one

    c. Between Jupiter and Saturn   d. Between Mars and Jupiter

3. What is a Light Year?

    a. The distance light travels from the Sun to Earth

    b. The distance light travels in one year

    c. The time it takes light to travel from one end of the universe to the other

    d. A cool, refreshing drink with few calories

4. What galaxy is our solar system in?

    a. Adromeda   b. NGC 4414

    c. Milky Way   d. Three Musketeers

5. List two ancient monuments whose construction was associated with the solar cycle.

    1. _____   2. _____

6. Aristotle believed the Earth was round because a traveler moving south saw new stars that had been hidden below the _____

    a. ocean's waves   b. sun's disk

    c. southern horizon   d. tree-tops

7. Who calculated the circumference of the earth in 200 BC?

    a. Pythagoras   b. Aristotle

    c. Aristarchus   d. Erastosthenes

8. In one or two sentences explain how he (the person in #7 above) determined the circumference of the earth.

_____

_____

_____

(Homework) From Signs & Seasons Textbook; Prologue, the Sky Above

9. Matching

Greater light that rules the day	seasons
Lesser light that rules the night	year
Collective name for the two great lights	month
Star groupings	day
Single cycle of light & dark	constellations
A complete lunar (moon) cycle	sun
Cycle of weather changes	moon
Sun's complete cycle	luminaries

10. According to Jewish tradition, who was an astronomer?
      a. Abraham   b. Noah
      c. Jacob   d. Moses

11. Which statement best describes *Classical Astronomy*?
      a. Astronomy used by the Hebrews and described in the Bible
      b. Astronomy that holds to the geocentric model proposed by Ptolemy
      c. Greek and Roman astronomy that continued into Christian Europe and America
      d. Astronomy based on the heliocentric model proposed by King James

12. Which statement is NOT true about the almanac?
      a. It will tell you the time of sunrise for every day of the year
      b. It went out of publication about the time of the American Revolution
      c. It provides positions of the planets throughout the year
      d. One popular almanac was printed in Philadelphia by B. Franklin

13. The heliocentric theory_____
      a. offers a better explanation of the movement of the planets
      b. is scriptural
      c. provides a thorough explanation for the study of astrophysics
      d. was the basis for the Egyptian calendar

14. T/F. Nowadays, time is no longer measured by the *Two Great Lights*.

15. Re-read the paragraph on page 8 that starts with the word 'Timekeeping.' Is JR's point true for you? Reply in one or two sentences. (2)

_____

_____

(Also in PLS Assignments)

Create a Backyard Compass

We're starting off the course with a fairly difficult time consuming activity.
Watch the video in Haiku Week 1
Instructions are also in the S&S textbook on pages 189 & 190.
If circumstances do not allow you to place paving stones in your yard:

     a. Can you paint your driveway or patio?

     b. Sidewalk chalk is the last resort; use it if you must.

Like most activities, post a picture or pictures in the drop-box and a paragraph sharing the experience of doing this.   What time was solar noon at your house?

This page blank on purpose.
You may doodle here.

Week 2 Review Questions

From Class

1. Why is it quite understandable for the ancients to believe the earth was the center of the universe? (2)

_____

2. What is retrograde motion?
   a. Stars going backwards
   b. Planets appearing to move west to east
   c. Planets appearing to move east to west
   d. Ptolemy's explanation of geocentrism

3. Whose geocentric model was used and accepted for centuries?
   a. Ptolemy   b. Aristotle   c. Aristarchus   d. Eratosthenes

4. How did Ptolemy explain the retrograde motion of planets?
   a. Parallax theory
   c. Ecliptic cycles
   c. Epicycles
   d. Celestial sphere cycles

5. In two or three sentences, explain what stellar parallax has to do with the history of astronomy. (3)

_____

_____

6. What ancient astronomer proposed a sun-centered universe?
   a. Aristotle   b. Copernicus   c. Aristarchus   d. Kepler

7. What assumption did Ptolemy make when stating his model?
   a. The planets revolve around the Sun
   b. The Earth is stationary
   c. The Moon revolves around the Sun
   d. The Moon is stationary

8. Why did astronomers have to keep adjusting Ptolemy's model?
   a. Ptolemy's original data were not translated accurately
   b. Something was fundamentally wrong with the model
   c. Measuring instruments improved constantly
   d. It didn't take centrifugal force into account

9. What type of model of the universe did Copernicus' religious beliefs push him to investigate?
   a. Earth-centered
   b. Gravity-centered
   c. Elliptical
   d. Sun-centered

10. What was the result of the tilting of the plane of Earth's equator, according to Copernicus?
      a. Earth's changing seasons   b. Changes in gravitational pull
      c. Changes in Moon phases   d. Sunspots

11. What was Copernicus able to calculate relatively accurately?
      a. The distance between Earth and the Moon
      b. The time required for Mercury to orbit the Sun
      c. The relative distances of planets from the Sun
      d. The distance from the Sun to the Earth

12. What did Copernicus believe was a planet's perfect path around the Sun?
      a. An ellipse   b. An epicycle
      c. A circle   d. A slightly flattened circle

13. What is one incorrect assumption Copernicus made in his model?
      a. The Earth remains in a fixed location
      b. Planets move at a constant speed
      c. Stellar parallax could not exist
      d. His predictions about planets' motion were accurate

14. What body or bodies orbited the Sun, according to Tycho Brahe?
      a. Earth only   b. Not Earth but the other planets
      c. The Moon   d. All the planets including Earth

15. What orbital shape did Kepler find best fit his data?
      a. Circle   b. Oval   c. Egg-shaped   d. Ellipse

16. What did Kepler's second law explain?
      a. The shape of a planet's orbit as it moves around the Sun
      b. Gravity
      c. A planet's speed as it moves around the Sun
      d. Solar energy

17. What happens to a planet's speed as it moves around the Sun?
      a. It speeds up when it is closer to the Sun
      b. It slows down when it is closer to the Sun
      c. It remains the same throughout its orbit
      d. It speeds up and slows down several times

18. What data do you need to tell a planet's average distance from the Sun, according to Kepler's third law?
      a. Approximate diameter and circumference of the planet
      b. Length of time a planet takes to orbit the Sun
      c. Gravitational pull of the planet
      d. Distance from Earth and the Moon

19. When comparing the Copernican and Ptolemaic models, Copernicus's pulls ahead of Ptolemy's in its' _____

20. T/F Copernicus believed that a heliocentric model would provide more accurate data for the Roman Catholic Church calendar, helping ensure that holy days were observed at the right time.

(Homework) From Signs & Seasons Textbook; Chapter 1: The Light He Called Day

21. What is likened unto a bridegroom?
    a. The Sun   b. Jesus   c. The Moon   d. The Heavens

22. What is the most basic unit for passage of time?
    a. The year   b. The moon cycles
    c. The day   d. Watching shadows

23. Imagine life before watches and clocks. (This is the bulk of human history.) How did people tell the time of day? (2)

_____

_____

24. What are the two parts of a sundial?   1. _____   2. _____

25. What book of the Bible mentions a sundial?
    a. Genesis   b. Isaiah   c. Ezekiel   d. Mathew

26. JR shows a picture of the first American coin on page 12. Who designed it? (The answer is not in the book; you'll have to look it up.) (3) _____

27. T/F. The sundial is marked to ascertain the 24 hours in a day.

28. What are the three similarities between a modern clock/watch and the sundial?

1. _____

2. _____

3. _____

29. T/F 'High Noon' and 'meridian' are similar terms but one is when you're looking south and the other is when you're looking north.

30. Where did we get AM and PM and what do the initials mean? (2)

_____

31. Why wouldn't 'noon' (12:00) on the clock in our homes perfectly match up the true 'high noon'?
        a. Because we have no way of knowing what the real high noon is
        b. Because we set our clock to a specific time zone so everyone lives on a standard time.
        c. Because high noon only occurs four times a year
        d. Because out clocks are linked to a GPS signal

32. T/F. In the summertime the sun lights half the earth; but in the wintertime less than half.

33. What is the terminator? (2)

_____

34. Why is it that when we look up and see light, (blue sky, clouds) but when astronauts in outer space look up, they see black. (2)

_____

35. How many times a day do we experience twilight?
        a. Once at Sunset   b. Once at Sunrise
        c. Twice   d. Four times

36. Explain why the Far East is also called the *Orient* and Europe used to be called the *Occident*? (3)

_____

_____

37. T/F. For navigation, the *four principle directions*, *cardinals* and *compass points* all have the same meaning.

38. For those of us in the northern hemisphere, the sun always hangs in the _____
        a. South   b. North   c. East   d. West

39. Examine the orientation of your house and explain to me what part gets the rising sun, the setting sun and what part has a southern exposure and gets the sun all day long. (3)

_____

_____

_____

41. What does JR explain as the 'limit of our vision'?
      a. the meridian   b. astronomy   c. the horizon   d. *neutrinos*

Week 2 Activity
(Also in PSL Assignments)

Draw an Ellipse

I know you're probably still working on your lawn compass; but this is an easy assignment. ***Draw an ellipse*** per the instructions below. Take a picture and put it in the drop-box. Show your tacks, pencil and string as well as the ellipse. (Also read the explanation at the bottom of this page)

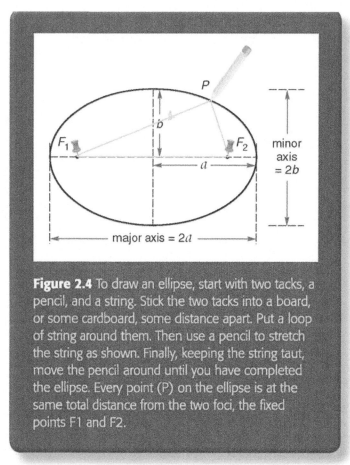

Figure 2.4 To draw an ellipse, start with two tacks, a pencil, and a string. Stick the two tacks into a board, or some cardboard, some distance apart. Put a loop of string around them. Then use a pencil to stretch the string as shown. Finally, keeping the string taut, move the pencil around until you have completed the ellipse. Every point (P) on the ellipse is at the same total distance from the two foci, the fixed points F1 and F2.

To get a little more precise: An ellipse is *a geometrical shape of which every point (P) is the same total distance from two fixed points, or foci.* ("Foci" is the plural of focus.) A circle is a set of points in a given plane at a certain distance from a given center. An ellipse is thus a somewhat more complex shape, defined with reference to two points (the foci), instead of one (Figure 2.4). (When you move the two foci closer to each other, the shape becomes more circular. When the foci lie on top of each other, the shape is a circle.) The farther apart the two foci of an ellipse are, the more "eccentric" it is said to be, and the more elongated it is. The planets' orbits are not actually all that eccentric. But they aren't perfect circles, either, and realizing this was Kepler's first major achievement.

Week 3 Review Questions

1. What belief caused people to be unsettled by Galileo's observations?
   - a. Perfection of the heavens
   - b. Earth as the center of the universe
   - c. Astrology as a science
   - c. Understanding gravity, light & matter

2. What did Galileo discover about the surface of the Sun, by using his telescope?
   - a. The Sun's surface supports the "perfection of the heavens"
   - b. The Sun's surface is hotter than previously believed
   - c. The Sun's surface has relatively dark spots
   - d. The Sun is solid, just as Earth is solid

3. T/F. Jupiter and its moons are like a miniature solar system.

4. What did the position of Jupiter's moons suggest to Galileo about their orbital plane?
   - a. Parallel with Venus's orbital plane
   - b. Similar to that of Mars
   - c. Each moon's orbital plane was different
   - d. Aligned with that of Earth

5. T/F. Venus's full phase occurs when its entire sunlit hemisphere is visible.

6. What really convinced Galileo that the Sun was at the center of the Solar System?
   - a. Jupiter's moons
   - b. The phases of the Moon
   - c. Venus's phases
   - d. Shape of Earth's orbit

7. That Jupiter could revolve around the Sun without losing its moons contradicted the theory that Earth must be _____ or it would lose its Moon.

8. What was Galileo's punishment for advocating a heliocentric solar system? (2)

_____

9. What did Newton's first law of motion say about an object in motion, in the absence of force?
   - a. The object will gradually slow down and stop
   - b. The object will tend to stay in motion
   - c. The object will stop suddenly
   - d. The object will accelerate in speed

10. What did Newton's third law of motion deal with?
   - a. Inertia
   - b. Acceleration
   - c. Gravity
   - d. Actions and reactions

11. What makes the idea of curvature of space so difficult to understand?
      a. There is no practical illustration of the theory on Earth
      b. The idea requires imagining the world in two dimensions
      c. The human brain has not evolved enough to think this way
      d. The idea makes you think in terms of more than three dimensions

12. What have technological advances since Einstein's time allowed scientist to confirm repeatedly about light?
      a. The speed of light varies with gravitational pull
      b. Light waves neither bend nor curve
      c. Light moves more slowly than Newton thought
      d. The constancy of the speed of light

(Homework) From Signs & Seasons Textbook; Chapter 2: The Darkness He Called Night

13. JR mentions the **Milky Way** on page 29; do you have any idea what it is? Have you ever seen it? Now do a web search of what it is and summarize it here in one or two sentences. (3)

_____

_____

14. JR then talks about light pollution. How would you rate the light pollution where you live? Use a scale of 1 to 10, 10 being so bad you're lucky to see any stars at all, 1 being you live in a remote country setting, no street lights and city lights are a long way off. Explain your rating. (2)

_____

15. What occupation does the text mention as being quite knowledgeable of most aspects of astronomy? _____

16. Either from the text or looking it up, explain the difference between a constellation and an asterism. Give three examples of each. (3)

_____

_____

_____

_____

17. What is so special about the North Star? What's its other name? Explain its' connection with the big and little dipper. (3)

_____

_____

_____

18. When can you see *Orion's Belt*?
    a. Spring   b. Summer   c. Fall   d. Winter

19. What is the brightest star in the sky?
    a. Sirius   b. Canis Major   c. Betelgeuse d. Polaris

20. What Greek poet described the ancient constellations? _____

21. There were 48 original constellations; how many are there now? _____

22. Which statement is ***false*** concerning the celestial sphere?
        a. It has no physical reality, but it serves as a useful model
        b. It represents a way of thinking about or viewing the stars and planets
        c. We can use it to determine distances to stars
        d. It's like a gigantic dome and the stars are on the inside ceiling

23. What was used before planetariums came along to depict motions of celestial objects?

_____

24. Would the night sky look any different if you were viewing it from Saturn? Why or why not? (2)

_____

_____

25. Pages 41-44 discuss the rolling of the sphere. Read it, but I will also teach it in class. Once you understand why the stars move from east to west each evening and why Polaris doesn't move at all, explain it to someone in your house. Did you? Who? (3) _____

26. From the picture on the bottom of page 47, explain to me (in your own words) meridian and zenith. Do we all have our own meridian or is the meridian for someone in Ohio the same as mine here in New York? Why or why not? (3)

_____

_____

_____

27. T/F. The celestial equator is like imagining earth's equator projected straight up onto dome of the celestial sphere.

From the Lawn Compass Activity

28. Approximately which direction would a shadow in the morning point?
     a. North   b. South   c. East   d. West

29. Approximately which direction would a shadow in the middle of the day point?
     a. North   b. South   c. East   d. West

30. When the sun is passing through your meridian, what time is it? (2)

_____

Week 3 Activity
Looking North

This is our first star gazing activity. In this week's reading JR discusses the northern sky on pp.31,32; and I talked about it in class as well.

This will be a tough assignment if you have a lot of light pollution in your area. You may have to talk to your parents/guardian about getting out of town on the first clear sky opportunity.

1. Find your latitude. (If you need help doing this, call, text or email me.) Your latitude on earth is equivalent to the altitude (height above horizon) of Polaris.   Use your lawn compass and look north.

2. Now you're ready to see all things north. **Find the big dipper, the North Star and Cassiopeia.** Try really, really hard to see the Little Dipper.   The stars in the little dipper are of low magnitude and very difficult to see.   Let me know if you have any success here.

3. Show someone in your family these three items and write me the story of your whole experience.

This page blank on purpose

You may doodle here

Week 4 Review Questions

From Class

1. What can you reasonably guess if you know the density of a celestial object?
   a. Circumference of the object's orbit
   b. Composition of the object
   c. Time elapsed for one full orbit by the object
   d. Distance of the object from the Sun

2. Ordinary surface rocks weigh about _____ per cubic centimeter.
   a. 1 gram   b. 3 grams   c. 5.5 grams   d. 6 grams

3. Earth's outer layer is the _____
   a. Inner core   b. Outer core   c. Mantle   d. Crust

4. Matching:

Measures how much matter is in a given space	Outer core
Just beneath the crust, hot but not liquid	Inner core
Thick liquid made of iron and nickel	Earth
Thick solid made of iron and nickel	Oblate spheroid
12,800 km in diameter	Density
Bulged like water slopping over the sides of a spinning bowl	Mantle

5. T/F. Earth's average density is 5.5 grams per cubic centimeter.

6. T/F. We learn about Earth's interior by drilling deep holes in the surface hundreds of kilometers into the crust.

7. T/F. Surface rocks are eight times denser than water.

8. What is Earth's atmosphere mostly made up of?
   a. Oxygen and carbon dioxide   b. Oxygen and water vapor
   c. Oxygen and ozone   d. Oxygen and nitrogen

9. What percentage of Earth's atmosphere is Nitrogen Molecules?
   a. 50   b. 21   c. 1   d. 78

10. What is the lowest level of the Earth's atmosphere called?
    a. Stratosphere   b. Mesosphere
    c. Troposphere   d. Thermosphere

11. The rainbow of visible light is part of a full range of radiation called the _____ _____.

12. What does the ozone layer of the Earth's atmosphere do?
    a. Creates a toxic zone for astronauts   b. Causes corrosion of metals on Earth
    c. Filters UV radiation   d. Depletes the stratosphere

13. T/F. The greenhouse effect raises the atmosphere's temperature too high for living organisms.

14. Matching

A region of space where magnetic forces can be detected	Aurora
Doughnut-shaped rings of charged particles around the Earth	Magnetic field
Light radiated in the upper atmosphere because of impacts from charged particles	Van Allen radiation belts
Different location from magnetic north pole; exact top of Earth	True North

15. Which statement below about magnetic north is accurate?
   a. It is the same as the geographic North Pole
   b. It can wander hundreds of miles
   c. It is the northern region of a giant bar magnet within the Earth
   d. It is the same as the geographic South Pole due to a reversal

16. Where do the charged particles in the Van Allen Belts mainly come from?
   a. Meteorites   b. Comets
   c. Sun   d. Outer space

17. What types of particles are trapped in the outer radiation belts?
   a. Neutrons   b. Protons
   c. Electrons   d. Atoms

18. What is the South Atlantic Anomaly (SAA) the result of?
   a. A bulge in the magnetic field   b. An ozone hole
   c. An area with much less radiation   d. A dip in the magnetic field

19. What is the effect of the South Atlantic Anomaly (SAA)
   a. People weigh less in the area
   b. Communication with satellites is hampered there
   c. Airplanes experience turbulence there
   d. UV rays are weaker in the area

(Homework) From S&S Textbook; Chapter 3: The Circle of the Month

20. When we follow the cycle of the Moon's phases from night to night, we are actually observing the Moon at different positions in its _____.

21. How long does it take the moon to pass through all its' phases?
   a. 29.5   b. 31, but sometimes 30   c. 7   d. 27

22. How many different types of calendars does JR mention on p.56?
   a. 3   b. 2   c. 1   d. 0

23. How is a New Moon depicted on a wall calendar? _____

24. What did God command the Israelites to burn on each New Moon?
    a. Two turtle doves   c. A partridge
    c. Incense   d. Four Calling Birds

25. When (in days of the moon's cycle) do you see a waxing crescent Moon? _____

26. Explain 'Earthshine.' (2)
_____

27. Approximately how many days does it take the Moon to move from New Moon to 1st Quarter Moon?
    a. 3   b. 4   c. 7   d. 14

28. The sun just went down and it's dark enough to see the moon; if it's a 1st Quarter Moon, where would it be in the sky? (3) _____

29. What does gibbous mean? _____

30. T/F. The picture in the upper left on p.61 is a waning gibbous moon.

31. Can the light from the Moon cast a shadow? When would it cast the strongest shadow?
_____

32. What would have been the phase of the Moon the night before Jesus' crucifixion? (2)
_____

33. At New Moon the Sun and the Moon rise and set together; three days later, how many minutes after sunrise will the moon rise? (3) _____

34. T/F. You can tell if the moon is waning or waxing by observing which side (east or west) of the moon is lit.

35. What does waning mean? _____

36. What is halfway between a Full Moon and a New Moon (going from a full moon)?
_____

Week 4 Activity

Sun Azimuth & Elevation

Where does the sun rise and set? No.... really, where precisely does it rise and set? Does it change? If so, why and what effect does that change have on us?

Once we know where it rises and sets, what path does it take across the sky? Where is the sun at noon?

In this week's backyard astronomy, you'll learn about the apparent movement of the sun over your world.

1. Watch the videos on week 4a

2. Complete the worksheets on the next page.

3. There will be *three* things to put in the dropbox:
    a. The attached worksheets (2 pages)
    b. A picture of you doing azimuth
    c. A picture of you doing elevation

Have fun doing this; call if you need help. 315-723-3384 (or leave a text to have me call you)

Week 4 Worksheet (p.1)

Azimuth: The Basic Idea.   You will be placing 10 dots in the diagram below on the blue band. The top blue band represents the horizon looking East, the bottom blue band is the horizon looking West. Each dot renders the Sun's rising and setting azimuth for five specific dates as follows:

> March 20th - Vernal Equinox
> June 21st - Summer Solstice
> Week 4 - The day you take your compass reading
> September 22nd – Autumnal Equinox
> December 21st – Winter Solstice

Azimuth: Specific Instructions. For the Week-4 position, do what I did on the video and get a real reading on your compass.   For the other data points, go to http://www.timeanddate.com/sun/usa/syracuse   It might take a few minutes, but learn how to change the chart to your nearest big city and how to change the month/year.   Then examine the table and find where it identifies the sunrise & sunset azimuth for each appointed day.

Place the 10 dots representing each date on the blue bands. Draw a line from each dot and identify it. (Once you have a degree, draw a line from the center of the compass through the appropriate degree, then out to and beyond your dot.)

Week 4 Worksheet (p.2)

Elevation: The Basic Idea. You will be placing 5 dots on the diagram below just outside the protractor. The base of the protractor represents the ground/horizon; the degrees lines help you plot the altitude of the Sun at noon. Each dot renders the Sun's altitude for those same five dates as in the azimuth exercise:

Elevation: Specific Instructions. For the Week-4 position, do what I did on the video and get a real reading on your protractor. For the other data points, go to the same website http://www.timeanddate.com/sun/usa/syracuse Look in the Solar noon column.

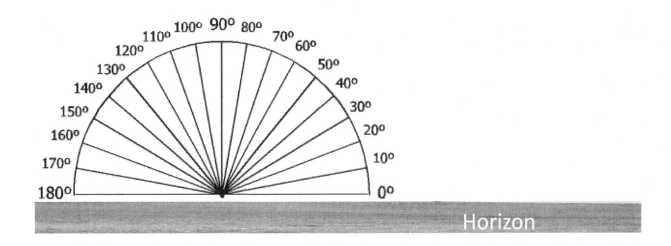

Answer these questions.

1. Is there a day or a time of year when you think you can stand outside at noon and not cast a shadow? YES NO Why or why not?

_____

2. On what day(s) would you expect daylight to be 12 hours long? _____

3. Consider what you have done in this lab. What is going on here? Write a brief explanation of why the Sun's azimuth and elevation change.

_____

_____

_____

Week 5 Review Questions

From Class

1. How far is the Moon from Earth?

    a. 180,500 miles   b. 212,500 miles   c. 240,000 miles   d. 327,000 miles

2. T/F. The Moon's diameter is almost one-half the size of Earth's diameter.

3. List the two principal features of the moonscape.

    _____   _____

4. What almost completely covers the Moon's far side?

    a. Craters   b. Volcanoes   c. Dry Ice   d. Lava

5. When does the Moon appear to be larger?

    a. At its apogee   b. During neap tides

    c. At its perigee   d. During autumn tides

6. Viewing from above the North Pole, what direction does the moon rotate around the earth?

    a. Clockwise   b. Counter-clockwise

7. How long does it take the earth to wobble once? _____

8. Does the spinning of earth having anything to do with tides?

    a. Yes   b. No

9. Which object has the greatest effect on earth's tides?

    a. Sun   b. Moon   c. Mars   d. Earth

10. T/F. The Sun is so far away, it has no effect on earth's tides.

11. What happens when the Sun and the Moon line up with Earth, near the times of a full or new moon?

    a. Neap tides   b. Tidal friction   c. Precession   d. Spring tides

12. What happens when the moon is at a right angle to the earth/sun?

    a. Neap tides   b. Tidal friction   c. Precession   d. Spring tides

13. Spring tides and neap tide levels are about _____ % higher or lower than average.

14. T/F. High and low tides are the same all over the world; about 7 feet.

15. How many times do the tides come in and then go out in one 24 hour period? _____

16. Explain Penumbra and Umbra. (3) _____

_____

(Homework) From Week 4 Activity on the Sun's Azimuth & Elevation

17. Matching for Azimuth Sunrise in North America

Vernal & Autumnal Equinox	Very Low in the sky
Summer Solstice	Due East (90 degrees)
Winter Solstice	Very High in the sky

18. Matching for Sun's elevation at noon in North America

Vernal & Autumnal Equinox	~37 degrees
Summer Solstice	~84 degrees
Winter Solstice	~61 degrees

19. For people living in North America, when would you not cast a shadow at noon?
   a. Summer Solstice   b. Winter Solstice
   c. Vernal Equinox   d. You would **always** cast a shadow

(Homework) From S&S Textbook; Chapter 4: The Tabernacle for the Sun

20. From day to day, how noticeable is the sun's apparent position in the sky? (2)

_____

21. The ecliptic is the path the sun takes, an eclipse is the moon blocking the sun; are these two words related to one-another? Explain. (2)

_____

22. T/F. The constellations are connected to the seasons.

23. Why do we see the sun and all the planets somewhere near the ecliptic? (2)

_____

24. What are the constellations called that are on the ecliptic? How many are there?

_____

25. What is the connection, language wise, between the zodiac and scripture? (2)

_____

26. What two people in Bible could have taught you this course instead of me? (2)

_____

27. In three or four sentences, summarize JR's point about astronomy and astrology on pp. 78 & 79. (3)

_____

_____

_____

28. Explain the relationship between the celestial equator and the ecliptic. (3)

_____

_____

29. I think the last paragraph on p.81 is a key concept for this book and this course. Read it ten times and copy it word for word here. (3) _____

_____

_____

_____

30. List the 12 constellations of the zodiac in order; start with Virgo and go east. (3)

1._____ 2._____ 3._____ 4._____

5._____ 6._____ 7._____ 8._____

9._____ 10._____ 11._____ 12._____

31. List any five stars in the zodiac and tell me what constellations they are in. (3)

     1._____ _____

     2._____ _____

     3._____ _____

     4._____ _____

     5._____ _____

Week 5 Activity

Tides Look-up

1. Choose a major city on any coast. (Maybe the one nearest you.) _____

2. Using a calendar or computer, find the next dates for each of the major phases of the moon and put them in column 2 below.

3. Complete column 4 by finding the height of each high tide for the location you chose and the dates in column 2. (web search)

Col 1	Col 2	Col 3	Col 4
1st Quarter	Date: _____	High Tide (ft)	
		High Tide (ft)	
Full Moon	Date: _____	High Tide (ft)	
		High Tide (ft)	
3rd Quarter	Date: _____	High Tide (ft)	
		High Tide (ft)	
New Moon	Date: _____	High Tide (ft)	
		High Tide (ft)	

4. Which phase had the highest tides? _____

5. Why? _____

6. Put this completed page in the drop-box.

Week 6 Review Questions

From Class

1. What constellation will October's (2017) full moon be in?
   - a. Aquarius
   - b. Cetus
   - c. Gemini
   - d. Pisces

2. What did Hermann von Helholtz and Lord Kelvin propose was the source of the Sun's energy in the mid-19th century?
   - a. Nuclear fission
   - b. Gravitational contraction
   - c. Nuclear fusion
   - d. Large diffuse cloud

3. What theory prompted scientists to consider that mass can be converted to energy and vice versa, and that this process could be the source of the Sun's energy?
   - a. Contraction theory
   - b. Fusion theory
   - c. Theory of equilibrium
   - d. Special Theory of relativity

4. What did Hans Bethe's theory propose is the primary source of the Sun's energy?
   - a. Nuclear fission
   - b. Helium nucleus
   - c. Nuclear fusion
   - d. Orbiting electrons

5. Where on the Sun are the temperature and density of hydrogen great enough to support fusion?
   - a. Corona
   - b. Solar core
   - c. Convection Zone
   - d. Aurora

6. What force on the Sun balances the force of gravity?
   - a. Forces tending to expand the gas
   - b. Hydrostatic force
   - c. Nuclear fusion
   - d. Atoms

7. What method of energy transfer is related to the expression "heat rises"?
   - a. Conduction
   - b. Convection
   - c. Wavelengths
   - d. Radiation

8. What is the principal means of energy transfer inside the Sun?
   - a. Conduction
   - b. Convection
   - c. Wavelengths
   - d. Radiation

9. What layer of the Sun is where solar flares and eruptions come from?
   - a. Photosphere
   - b. Chromosphere
   - c. Corona
   - d. Aurora

10. What layer of the Sun extends for hundreds of thousands of miles from the Sun and can be seen during solar total eclipses?
    - a. Photosphere
    - b. Chromosphere
    - c. Corona
    - d. Aurora

11. What particles, in addition to electrons, make up most of solar wind?
      a. Neutrons   b. Dust
      c. Comet tails   d. Protons

12. Which of the following is a dramatic effect of the solar wind that you can see near the Earth's poles?
      a. Auroras   b. Sunspots
      b. Solar flares   d. Radiation

13. Who discovered there is a fairly regular cycle in the number of sunspots and also found the sunspot cycle lasts about 11 years?
      a. Hermann von Helmholtz   b. Lord Kelvin
      c. Heinrich Schwabe   d. William Herschel

14. What can heat solar material to tens of millions of degrees in just a few seconds?
      a. Auroras   b. Sunspots
      c. Solar flares   d. Radiation

15. What makes up more than 99 percent of the Solar System's mass?
      a. Jupiter   b. The Sun
      b. Solar gas   d. Solar dust

(Homework) From Week 5 Activity on Tides

16. This is a thinking question; you can look it up or just guess. When the moon is over the ocean, it tugs on the water and makes it rise. Does it happen right away, or does the high tide lag behind a little? (2)

_____

(Homework) From Signs & Seasons Textbook; Chapter 5: The Circle of the Bear

17. What are the four astronomical occurrences that mark the changing seasons? (See Bottom of p. 93)

    _____   _____

    _____   _____

18. How can you tell what constellations the sun is passing through during the daytime? (3)

_____

_____

19. Tell me four things about the vernal equinox. (2)

    (1) _____

    (2) _____

    (3) _____

    (4) _____

20. Why do we have daylight savings time whereby we set our clocks forward one hour? (2)

_____

_____

21. Why do things start warming up in May? (2) _____

_____

22. T/F. For those living in the United States; the further north you live, the longer your summer days will be.

23. Provide the word origins of 'solstice' and 'tropic.' (2)

_____

_____

24. Where would you have to be on June 21st in order to cast no shadow at noon? (3)

_____

25. What is JR's main point about July? (2) _____

_____

26. In the northern hemisphere the longest day with the most direct sunlight is June 21st; why ***isn't*** late June the hottest time of the year? (2)

_____

_____

27. How many times, in one year, does the sun rise and set precisely East and West? _____

28. Who might you see flying south in September?
    a. Pigs   b. Geese   c. Old people   d. Bees

29. T/F. The armillary sundial is inferior to the gnomon style sundial.

30. How long ago did earthlings adopt standard time zones? Why? (3) _____

_____

_____

31. What constellation would be obscured by the Sun in November? _____

32. Tell me four things about the winter solstice. (3)

      (1) _____

      (2) _____

      (3) _____

      (4) _____

33. What is the coldest month of the year? _____

Week 6 Activity

Autumn Equinox & Declination

This week has the autumn equinox in it, one of the four important astronomical days each year. So our activity will involve checking east-west bearings.   Even though the actual date is

September 22, take advantage of any sunny day this week ……. Close enough.

1. Let's check out the accuracy of your lawn compass; stand on it at sunrise and see if your shadow points directly west. Or stand there at sunset and see if it points directly east.   Early in the morning and late in the day, you cast long shadows. Wouldn't it be neat if your shadow was actually over the west or east marker? ***Put a picture of you doing this in the drop-box.***

2. Many homes are built purposely to be compass aligned. The home I live in was built so the big living room windows faced due south. The idea is for the sun to help warm the house from sunrise to sunset all winter long. It works! Free heat! Check your house out; is it compass aligned? ***Put what you discovered in the drop-box.***

3. Many towns and cities designed their streets to run exactly east-west & north-south. Using Google-Earth I zoomed in on Syracuse NY. I learned the major two highways are more aligned with a local river and the general lay of the land.   But the vast majority of the city streets were near perfectly aligned east-west, north-south.   ***Check out a town or city near you and tell me about it…….. in the drop-box.***

4. Now let's turn our attention to the compass and learn how far off it is. Just for fun you can see if you notice any error in your compass by pointing it at the rising sun and see if it reads exactly east.   There probably isn't enough precision to see that it is off.

   a. Go to the noaa.gov website where you'll see the Magnetic Declination Map I used in class (http://www.ngdc.noaa.gov/geomag/img/DeclinationMap_US.png)

   b. What is the magnetic declination for where you live? _____

   c. Do you have to add or subtract (Read fine print on web site) from the compass reading to come up with a "true" reading?

   d. Place the answer to b & c above in the drop-box.

This page blank on purpose

You may doodle here

Week 7 Review Questions

From Class

1. Which planet was named for the Roman god of commerce and travel?
    a. Mercury   b. Venus   c. Mars   d. Jupiter

2. What does the fact that Mercury's density is only slightly less than Earth's density mean?
    a. Mercury is still in the process of formation
    b. Mercury has a higher concentration of heavy elements
    c. Mercury has about the same mass as Earth
    d. Mercury's core is lighter than Earth's

3. What has puzzled scientists about Mercury?
    a. Evidence of volcanic activity   b. Its slow rotation and orbit
    c. Its magnetic field   d. Evidence of a sulfuric atmosphere

4. How many times does Mercury rotate during its orbital period?
    a. Two-thirds of one rotation   b. Once
    c. One and one-half times   d. Twice

5. What causes the Sun to exert a torque on Mercury?
    a. Tilt of its axis   b. Eccentric orbit
    c. One side more massive   d. Very dense interior

6. What is another name stargazers often use to refer to Venus?
    a. Morning and Evening Star   b. Goddess of Beauty
    c. Bright Star   d. Sunset Star

7. What on Earth has a similar composition to the surface rocks of Venus?
    a. Magnetized rocks   b. Basaltic volcanic rock
    c. Sedimentary rocks   d. Crystalline quartz rocks

8. What have scientists not found on Venus?
    a. Dense interior   b. Volcanic activity
    c. Craters   d. Magnetic field

9. How long does Venus's orbit around the Sun take?
    a. 98 days   b. 117 days   c. 225 days   d. 252 days

10. What planet, along with Venus, rotates in a clockwise fashion?
    a. Mercury   b. Earth   c. Uranus   d. Neptune

11. What covers about two-thirds of Venus's surface?
    a. Mountains   b. Craters   c. Volcanoes   d. Rolling hills

12. What makes up 96 percent of Venus's atmosphere?
    a. Nitrogen   b. Ozone   c. Carbon dioxide   d. Oxygen

13. When is the best time to see Mars from Earth?
    a. During Earth's winter solstice   b. When Mars is in opposition
    c. At the beginning of Earth's fall equinox   d. During Mars's summer

14. What gave scientists a negative answer to the question of whether there is life on Mars?
    a. Telescopic observations   b. Astronaut observations
    c. Earth probes   d. Occurrence of volcanic eruptions

15. What are the rocks on Mars rich in?
    a. Sulfur and silicon   b. Iron and silicon
    c. Iron and lead   d. Lead and sulfur

16. What erodes Mars' atmosphere and contributes to its loss of water?
    a. Solar winds   b. Sulfuric acid   c. Iron and sulfur   d. Gravitational pull

17. Which planet's day is almost the same length as Mars' day?
    a. Venus   b. Saturn   c. Earth   d. Jupiter

18. What season occurs in Mars' northern hemisphere when the planet is closest to the Sun?
    a. Spring   b. Summer   c. Fall   d. Winter

19. How many miles high is Olympus Mons?
    a. 5 miles   b. 10 miles   c. 15 miles   d. 20 miles

20. What color is Mars' surface, as seen in the first close-up photos?
    a. Yellowish   b. Red   c. Tan   d. Dark brown

21. Matching

Orbits the Sun in a more-circular orbit than any other planet?	Mercury
Hardest to see from Earth with the naked eye?	Earth
Scientists noticed seasonal changes?	Venus
The only planet with just one moon	Mars

22. T/F. Venus is the fastest planet in the Solar System.

23. T/F. Mercury's orbit is the least eccentric of the eight planets.

24. T/F. Venus is never seen farther than 46 degrees from the Sun.

(Homework) From Week 6 Activity on Tides & Magnetic Declination

25. T/F. There are some places in the United States where magnetic north and true north are the same.

26. T/F. The east-west compass readings matches the imaginary latitude lines.

(Homework) From Signs & Seasons Textbook; Chapter 6: The Seasonal Skies

. Tell me three things about 'magnitude:' Who first categorized the stars by magnitude? When? What scale did he use? (2)

. Fill in the table. List 15 1st magnitude stars; the constellation they are in and the season it can be seen in. (9)

	1st Magnitude Stars	Constellation	Season
1			
2			
3			
4			
5			
6			
7			
8			
9			
10			
11			
12			
13			
14			
15			

. Matching (2)

First appearance before sunrise	Temporal Rising
Rises visibly in night sky	Heliacal
Rises unseen behind daylight sky	Cosmic Rising

3 . Teach the chart on the cover of this workbook to someone in your family. How did the lesson go? (4) _____

Week 7 Activity

The Moon's Movement and Phases

You're going to plot the location of the moon over time in order to see for yourself its' orbit. The arc below represents the apparent path of the moon.

1. Pick a precise time that you will observe the moon over successive evenings. It is critical you plot it at the exact same time each evening.

2. Plot the moon on the arc with a pretty small circle and tag that dot with the date.

3. Do the same thing for as many evenings this week as possible.

Time _____

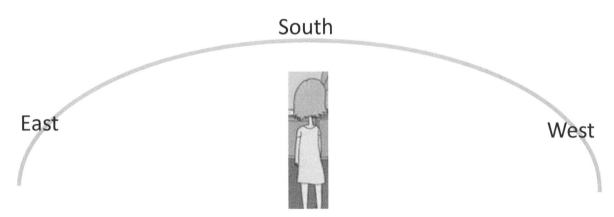

South

East

West

5. What is the moon doing this week? (circle one)   Waning   Waxing

6. Looking down from the North Pole, what direction does the moon orbit the earth?
Clockwise   or   Counterclockwise

7. Can you give me a good educated estimate of how many degrees the moon moves in a 24 hour period? (circle one)

    a. 5 degrees   b. 13 degrees   c. 21 degrees   d. 32 degrees)

Week 8

1. What is another ancient name for Jupiter?

a. The Eye Planet
b. The North Star
c. A Wandering Star
d. Jeopardy

2. What is Jupiter named for?

a. A Greek Goddess
b. Roman King of gods
c. Neptune's Son
d. An Egyptian God

3. How much bigger is Jupiter's diameter than Earth?
a. 11
b. 111
c. 10
d. 100

4. What is 90% of Jupiter's make-up?
a. Helium
b. Hydrogen
c. Water
d. Ammonia

5. What did the video say was probably at Jupiter's core?
a. Solid Rock
b. Liquid Lava
c. Water
d. More Gas

6. How long does it take for J. to Rotate once?
a. 24 Hours
b. 24 Days
c. 10 Hours
d. 10 D

7. Jupiter's various levels of clouds make it_____.
a. Black Looking
b. Attract Moons
c. Spin Faster
d. Colorful

8. T/F. Amazingly, Jupiter radiates more energy than it receives from the sun.

9. How does Jupiter make life possible on Earth?

    a.   It helps warm the earth

    b.   It deflects asteroids

    c.   It's moon's collect radiation

    d.   It supplies Hydrogen to us

10. At last count, how many moons does J. have?

    a.   36

    b.   360

    c.   63

    d.   630

11 What NASA spacecraft circled J for 8 years?

    a. Copernicus

    b. Einstein

    c. Cassini

    d. Galileo

12. What NASA spacecraft was launched to J. in 2011?

    a. Copernicus

    b. Einstein

    c. Juno

    d. Galileo

13. Starting from the Sun, what number planet is S.?

    a. 4

    b. 5

    c. 6

    d. 7

14. What Roman god is Saturn named after?

    a. Harvest

    b. Oceans

    c. Mountains

    d. Travelers

15. Who first discovered the Rings of Saturn?

    a. Copernicus

    b. Occam

    c. Galileo

    d. Hubble

16. Like J. and the sun, S's atmosphere is compromised mostly of what element?

    a. Helium

    b. Hydrogen

    c. Water

    d. Ammonia

17. T/F. 17. Also like Jupiter, Saturn emits more energy than it gets from the sun.

18. J. rotates in 10 Hours, how long is S.'s rotation?

    a. Same as Jupiter

    b. Faster; 9 hrs 30 min

    c. Slightly slower, 10hrs 33 min

    d. Same as Earth

19. Y/N. Does S. have rainstorms, snowstorms and even lightning?

20. How thick are Saturn's rings?
    a. A few miles
    b. A few meters
    c. A few feet
    d. A few inches

21. How long does it take for S. to orbit the Sun?
    a. 29.5 Years
    b. 2.95 Years
    c. 295 Years
    d. 12 Months

22. What is the latest count for Saturn's moons?
    a. 63
    b. 60
    c. 50
    d. 40

23. What is Saturn's largest Moon?
    a. Ganymede
    b. Europa
    c. Moon
    d. Titan

24. What NASA spacecraft is exploring S. and it's moons?
    a. Cassini
    b. Galileo
    c. Hubble
    d. Orion

25. Jupiter rotates in 10 Hours, Saturn in 10Hrs 33 Min How long for Uranus?
    a. Same as Jupiter
    b. Faster; 7 hrs 30 min
    c. Slower, 18 Hrs
    d. Same as Saturn

26. Y/N. Can Uranus be seen in the night sky?

27. When was Uranus recognized as a planet?
    a. 1781
    b. 1881
    c. 1981
    d. 1871

28. Where did Uranus get its' name?
    a. Egypt
    b. Greece
    c. Rome
    d. England

29. How long does it take Uranus to orbit the Sun?
    a. 84 years
    b. 8.4 years
    c. 84 years
    d. 840 years

30. Which statement is correct about Uranus?
    a. The 2nd largest planet 5 times the size of Earth
    b. The 2nd largest planet 4 times the size of Earth
    c. The 3nd largest planet 2 times the size of Earth
    d. The 3nd largest planet 4 times the size of Earth

31. What is the latest count for Uranus's moons?
    a. 27
    b. 60
    c. 50
    d. 40

32. What do scientist think is inside Uranus?
    a. Gold
    b. Silver
    c. Diamonds
    d. Emeralds

33. The small amount of Methane absorbs red light causing Uranus to look?
   a. Green
   b. Blue
   c. Red
   d. Yellow

34. What's unique about Uranus's angle of rotation?
   a. It's tilted 90 degrees
   b. It's tilted 180 degrees
   c. It's tilted 45 degrees
   d. It's tilted 22 degrees

35. What is similar between Saturn and Uranus?
   a. A Gas Planet
   b. Has a Solid Core
   c. Has Rings
   d. All of the Above

36. What NASA Spacecraft has visited Uranus?
   a. Cassini
   b. Voyager II
   c. Galileo
   d. Surveyor III

37. How was Neptune discovered?
   a. By the Voyager Spacecraft
   b. By observing a wobble in Uranus orbit
   c. Galileo's telescope
   d. The Hubble Telescope

38. Y/N. Does Neptune have Rings?

39. What is Triton?
   a. Another name for Neptune
   b. A Moon of Neptune
   c. A College
   d. A Ford Truck

40. What is Unique about Triton?
   a. It Rotates Backwards
   b. Has an Atmosphere
   c. It has Wrinkles
   d. All of the Above

41. What constellation is the center of the Milky Way Galaxy in?
   a. Sagittarius
   b. Pisces
   c. Gemini
   d. Virgo

From Signs & Seasons Textbook; Chapter 7: The Wandering Stars

42. What was Cicero (circa 50B.C.) referring to when he said: *"There is nothing more wonderful, nothing more beautiful."* _____

43. Match the Greek name with the Roman gods.

Phainon "The Shining Star"	*Zeus*
Phaethon "The Bright Star"	*Ares*
Pyrois "The Fiery Star"	*Hermes*
	Kronos
Stilbon "The Gleaming Star"	*Aphrodite*

44. Why do the planets shine brighter than even the brightest stars? (2)

_____

45. _____ planets are those that orbit the sun outside of Earth's orbit.

46. _____ planets are those that orbit the sun inside of Earth's orbit.

47. From my Saturn video, summarize its' travels. (3) _____

_____

48. List the only celestial objects brighter than Jupiter.(2)

49. From my Jupiter video, summarize its' travels (3) _____

_____

50. T/F. We see Mars at its brightest when it is on the opposite side of the Sun from us.

51. T/F. Since Venus and Mercury are both inferior planets; they are both easily seen near the sun; sometimes in the morning and sometimes in the evening.

Note: There are no questions from page 151 to the end of the chapter. This material will be taught when we study the Farmer's Almanac starting next week.

Week 8 Activity

The Milky Way

At the end of evening twilight, which now occurs at around 8:30 pm EDT, the splendor of this faint band of ghostly light may be seen bisecting the sky from southwest to northeast if you're well away from city lights. Directly overhead you'll find the three bright stars of the Summer Triangle, Vega, Deneb, and Altair, and if you look near the middle of these three stars you'll see the Milky Way appear to split into two distinct branches. The dark rift that seems to cause the split is actually part of the vast cloud of cool gas and dust that's distributed along the Galaxy's rotational plane, and it's blocking the light of more distant star clouds behind it

You have two weeks to do this activity. **I simply want you to take a nice long look at the Milky Way.** You might say: "wait a minute, I thought we live in, and are a part of, the Milky Way Galaxy, how do we see it if we're in it?" Yes, but we're on the outer reaches of it. Pretend you're a little gnat that just landed out near the edge of a frisbee and you've turned your head to look toward the center of the frisbee. When we're looking at this cool milky band in the sky, we're looking in toward the center of our home galaxy. Neat huh?

Your assignment.

1. Call a family meeting to discuss an early evening when you can be taken away from city lights. (If you live in the country, skip this step.) Be flexible in this meeting; allow 1 or 2 weeks to get on the family schedule. And yes, it needs to be a clear evening.

3. Try to find the Summer Triangle discussed in the paragraph and then find where the Milky Way splits into two distinct branches. (Having night-eyes might help.)

4. Put your story of this experience in the dropbox; a family viewing picture would be great.

Week 9 Review Questions

From Class

1. How big is Pluto?
   - a. Same size as our moon
   - b. Half the size of our moon
   - c. Twice the size of our moon
   - d. Same size as Earth

2. Why did Pluto get demoted?
   - a. It was too small
   - b. Its' orbit is funny
   - c. Failed one of the 3 requirements
   - d. Mickey and Minnie aren't planets

3. Who took pictures of Pluto?
   - a. Galileo
   - b. A British astronomer
   - c. The Hubble Telescope
   - d. Numerous Shuttle Astronauts

4. What did Clyde W. Tombaugh search for in the skies?
   - a. Small, faint disk
   - b. Signs of planetary motion
   - c. Planetesimals near Neptune
   - d. Dwarf stars

5. What is Pluto's status?
   - a. Protoplanet
   - b. Asteroid
   - c. Dwarf planet
   - d. Former comet

6. What is happening to the surface of Pluto?
   - a. Becoming more cratered
   - b. Contracting in size
   - c.. Developing new volcanoes
   - d. Getting warmer

7. What type of orbit are Pluto and Charon locked into?
   - a. Synchronous   b. Ecliptic   c. Spherical   d. Eccentric

8. T/F. Eris is two times more distant from the Sun than Pluto.

9. T/F. Pluto sometimes swings inside Neptune's orbit.

10. Where is the asteroid belt located?
    - a. Between Earth & Mars
    - b. Between Saturn & Uranus
    - c. Between Jupiter & Saturn
    - d. Between Mars and Jupiter

11. T/F. The asteroid belt is a crowded area in space.

12. What causes the gaps in the asteroid belt?
    - a. Europa's orbit
    - b. Jupiter's gravitational pull
    - c. Titan's gravitational pull
    - d. Comets sweeping through

13. T/F. Sir Isaac Newton first proposed that comets orbited the Sun.

14. What did Halley calculate?
    a. Orbits of several comets   b. Density of several comets
    c. Mass of several comets   d. Composition of several comets

15. T/F. Halley realized that one of the planets might affect the orbit of the comet through gravitational pull.

16. What is on the surface of a comet's nucleus?
    a. Frozen carbon dioxide   b. Crusty layer
    c. Water ice   d. Dirt

17. Where is the Oort cloud located?
    a. Far beyond Neptune's orbit   b. Between Uranus & Neptune
    c. Far beyond Eris's orbit   d. Between Neptune and Kuiper Belt

18. How long do short-period comets take to complete one orbit?
    a. Less than 150 years   b. Less than 200 years
    c. Greater than 250 years   d. Greater than 300 years

19. What is the term for an interplanetary chunk of matter that has struck a planet or a moon?
    a. Meteor   b. Fireball
    c. Meteorite   d. Asteroid

20. What Zodiac Signs would be impossible to see in Fall?
    a. Pisces & Capricorn   b. Capricorn & Libra
    b. Scorpio & Virgo   d. Libra & Virgo

21. What Zodiac Sign would you certainly see on Christmas Eve?
    a. Taurus   b. Libra   c. Scorpio   d. Capricorn

22. What Zodiac Sign would you see at midnight in the springtime?
    a. Capricorn   b. Libra   c. Virgo   d. Aquarius

From 2018 Farmers' Almanac

Note: because this booklet went to print before the 2018 Farmers' Almanac was published, these homework questions are available in Haiku Week 9.

Week 9 Activities
The Fall Zodiac

Along with some magnitude 1 stars and popular asterisms, it's time to start viewing and committing to memory the constellations of the zodiac. Let's start with the three zodiac signs most visible in October; we'll call them the fall constellations: Aquarius, Pisces & Aries. Even though six constellations are visible from sunset to sunrise, three of them are most easily in our gaze in the middle of the evening. Commit these three to memory, in order, as fall constellations; look at the night sky along the ecliptic and try to point them out. Make three flash cards or a small poster or anything to help you learn these three signs.

In the dropbox simply jot down a sentence or two of what you're doing to learn/memorize these.

Meteors

In class, we'll be looking at the *ANNUAL METEOR SHOWERS* chart in the *Farmers' Almanac*. I'll explain this homework assignment at that time.

This page blank on purpose

You may doodle here

Week 10 Review Questions

From Class

1. About how many stars make up the Milky Way Galaxy?
   a. 50 billion   b. 100 billion   c. 150 billion   d. 200 billion

2. What shape are most of the galaxy's stars arranged in?
   a. Spiral   b. Rectangular
   c. Globular   d. Parsec-shaped circle

3. What did William and Caroline Herschel and Jacobus Kapteyn conclude about the Sun's location in the galaxy?
   a. One-quarter of the way out from the center
   b. One-third to one half of the way out from the center
   c.. At the galaxy's center
   d. Near the galaxy's edge

4. From the northern hemisphere, what can you see beyond the Milky Way without a telescope?
   a. Andromeda Galaxy   b. Magellanic Clouds
   c. Numerous Super Stars   d. Exoplanets

5. What cast does a galaxy disk have as a whole?
   a. Yellowish   b. Reddish   c. Bluish   d. Whitish

6. What is packed more densely with stars, dust, and gas than any other part of the galaxy?
   a. The binary star system   b. The globular cluster
   c. The halo   d. The nuclear bulge

7. In what part of a spiral galaxy are globular clusters an important feature?
   a. The halo   b. The nuclear bulge
   c. The galaxy disk   d. The accretion disk

8. How big do scientists posit the galactic corona is in comparison to the radius of the galaxy disk and halo?
   a. Almost the same   b. Two times as big
   c. Two or three times as big   d. Four times as big

9. What tool do scientists use to see exoplanets?
   a. Radio waves   b. Infrared technology
   c. Hubble space telescopes   d. Non-optical telescopes

10. What clue implies the presence of a planet in a dust disk?
    a. Visual wobble   b. Collision among planetesimals
    c. Micolensing   d. Gaps in the dust

11. Which model of planet formation suggests that dense regions forming in the disk collect more and more material and suddenly collapse to form one or more planets?

    a. Gravitational pull   b. Core accretion
    c. Dusk-instability   d. Accretion disk

12. What is one of the numbers science uses to describe black holes?
    a. Mass   b. Size   c. Color   d. Texture

13. What property of a black hole demonstrates that as an object shrinks, its rotation rate speeds up?

    a. Neutrino   b. Gravitational pull
    c. Angular momentum   d. Microlensing

14. What has been providing important data to help astronomers tell the difference between black holes and other space phenomena?

    a. Radio waves   b. Orbiting X-ray observatories
    c. Non-optical telescope   d. Infrared technology

15. Which of the following is not used by scientists to observe the galactic nucleus?
    a. Satellite photos   b. Infrared/radio waves
    c. X-rays   d. Gamma rays

16. What does the massive-black-hole hypothesis seem to be the best explanation for?
    a. The Globular clusters   b. The Gravitational pull
    c. The Angular momentum   d. The Energy source in the Milky Way

17. T/F. Globular clusters pass through the disk twice during each orbit.

18. T/F. When a star seems to dim, that can be a sign of occultation---of a planet passing in front of the star and blocking the light.

19. T/F. Scientists expect that black holes do not have electric charges.

20. T/F. Because the gravitational field near a black hole would be so strong, any matter nearby would orbit very fast.

21. From memory or the cover of your workbook; what are the winter constellations?
    a. Aquarius, Libra, Pisces   b. Leo, Virgo, Libra
    b. Taurus, Gemini, Cancer   c. Pisces, Aries, Taurus

From 2018 Farmers' Almanac

Note: because this booklet went to print before the 2018 Farmers' Almanac was published, these homework questions are available in Haiku Week 10.

Week 10 Activities

The Winter Zodiac

Watch my week 10 video and memorize Taurus Gemini & Cancer. Just tell me you did it in the dropbox.

Finding Algol

Since this next week leads us up to Halloween, our backyard astronomy is ghoulish. A very unique star in the Constellation Perseus is called Algol. The name comes to us from Arabic for head of the ghoul, or head of the demon. The star changes its' brightness every three days and is in the middle of Medusa's forehead. Watch my video. Your assignment is to find and observe the star Algol two times. See if you can notice a difference in the brightness from the first observation to the second observation. Do this lab with a parent or guardian or sibling or friend and write your experience in the dropbox. Be sure and include the star patterns you used to find Algol.

This page blank on purpose

You may doodle here

Week 11 Review Questions

From Class

1. How is star brightness considered?
    a. Apparent & Spectral
    b. Apparent & Intrinsic
    c. Intrinsic & Spectral
    d. Absolute and Intrinsic

2. T/F. The smaller the magnitude number, the brighter the star.

3. Not counting the sun, what is the brightest star as viewed from earth?
    a. Vega
    b. Rigel
    c. Sirius
    d. Betelgeuse

4. Of the 15 brightest stars, which one is furthest away?
    a. Vega
    b. Rigel
    c. Sirius
    d. Betelgeuse

5. Do individual stars have their own "signature"?   What would you use to find it?

_____

6. Which of the following is NOT a major group of galaxies?

    a. Spiral
    b. Elliptical
    c. Barred
    d. Irregular

7. What type of galaxy is the Milky Way?
    a. Lenticular
    c. Elliptical Spiral
    b. Barred Spiral
    d. Irregular

8. How do scientists designate spiral galaxies that tend to have more gas and dust?
    a. Group a
    b. Group b
    c. Group c
    d. Group d

9. How do astronomers classify elliptical galaxies?
    a. By their diameter
    b. By their eccentricity
    c. By their density
    d. By their age

10. What type of galaxy tends to be small, with normally fewer than 25 percent as many stars in the Milky Way?
    a. Irregular
    b. Spiral
    c. Elliptical
    d. Lenticular

11. What did Halley discover about stars' motion in 1718?
    a. Some stars are fixed while others move
    b. Constellations' shapes remain the same over time
    c. Stars move with respect to one another
    d. Stars can only move if the galaxy moves

12. What may cause optical doubles to appear close?
    a. Sightlines
    b. Florescence
    c. Apparent magnitude
    d. Emission nebula

13. What type of clouds are wispier than their counterparts on Earth and spread over vast distances?
        a. Reflection clouds   b. Fluorescence clouds
        c. Emission nebulae clouds   d. Interstellar cirrus clouds

14. What was Jocelyn Bell searching for when she discovered pulsars?
        a. Dark matter   b. Quasars
        c. Dark nebula   d. Reflection nebula

15. What does hot dark matter primarily refer to?
        a. Dark energy   b. Dark nebula
        c. Neutrinos   d. Black holes

16. What are wavelengths directly related to?
        a. Energy levels   b. Apparent magnitude
        c. Luminosity   d. Florescence

17. What is an example of a type of wavelength that can cut through Earth's atmosphere to reach Earth's surface?
        a. Electromagnetic waves   b. Part of the radio spectrum
        c. Ultraviolet waves   d. Electromagnetic spectrum

18. What did Penzias and Wilson discover that led them to win the Nobel Prize in 1978?
        a. Electromagnetic spectrum   b. Dark matter
        c. Cosmic microwave background radiation   d. Pulsars

19. Which of Hubble's finding supported the big bang theory?
        a. The expanding universe   b. The value of X-ray observatories
        c. The existence of dark energy   d. The gravitational pull of galaxies

20. T/F. It is fairly easy for astronomers to tell from Earth what the shape of a given galaxy is.

21. T/F. Optical doubles are the same as binary star systems.

22. T/F. The dust and gas of the galaxies tend to clump together to form into interstellar clouds.

23. T/F. Electromagnetic waves include sending messages such as cell phone calls and television programs.

24. T/F. The sky is dark at night because the universe in infinite in size and age.

From Week 10 Activity Assignments

25. Read Acts 28:11; what winter constellation comes to mind?
    a. Taurus   b. Gemini   c. Cancer   d. Leo

26. What constellation is the star Algol in?
    a. Pisces   b. Algonquin   c. Perseus   d. Aquarius

From *The Astronomy of the Bible*, Chapter 1 (In this workbook pp.59-65)

27.1. M. begins by describing how the three tools of modern astronomy, the telescope, the spectroscope and the camera have advanced the science of Astronomy. What has each of these tools specifically done to increase our understanding? (3)

_____

_____

_____

28.2. What did Kepler and Newton bring to modern Astronomy? (2) _____

_____

_____

_____

29.3. How does M. explain the absence of astronomical information in the Bible? (3)

_____

_____

_____

30.4. Based on the information in the first four sections, construct a time-frame for Classical and

Modern Astronomy. How many years did astrology reign? (3)

_____

_____

_____

31.5. List six aspects of Astronomy figured out by the ancients. (3)

_____

_____

_____

32.6. T/F. M believes the O.T. can be used as an astronomy science textbook.

33.7. Which statement best summarizes M's point in section Seven? (3)
    a. The ancient Hebrews were superior artist and would have excelled in science had they not been so occupied in self-preservation.
    b. The ancient Hebrews was more interested in war and conquest and did not devote any energy toward scientific advancement.
    c. Isaiah was an astronomer as well as a prophet and writer
    d. The ancient Hebrews did not pursue the science of Astronomy because God forbade it as evil.

34.8. When did the ancient Hebrew have an opportunity to pursue scientific study? (2)

_____

_____

35.10. If Solomon was an ancient Einstein, why aren't his findings in the Bible? (3)

_____

_____

Week 11 Activities

The Spring Zodiac

Watch my week 11 video and memorize the spring constellations Leo, Virgo & Libra. Tell me you did it in the dropbox.

Finding The Planets

We've been looking at Stars, Asterisms and Constellations; now it's time to see the planets. Watch my week 11 video, wait for a clear sky, make a date with a family member and have an awesome viewing experience. Put your story in the drop-box.

This page blank on purpose

You may doodle here

Edward W. Maunder

Edward Walter Maunder (1851-1928) was a prominent British astronomer who was a Fellow of the Royal Astronomical Society, as well as founder and president of the British Astronomical Association. He was in charge of the Solar Department of the Greenwich Observatory and probably the outstanding authority on solar astronomy of his day. He authored many books, both technical and popular, including at least one book on the astronomy of the Bible, defending the Bible's accuracy and insights in astronomical matters. He served six years as Secretary of the Victoria Institute, the venerable British society for the defense of the Christian faith.

Excerpted from *Men of Science, Men of God* by Henry M. Morris. Copyright 1982, 1988 by Henry M. Morris. Used by permission.

Title: The Astronomy of the Bible
       An Elementary Commentary on the Astronomical References
            of Holy Scripture

Author: E. Walter Maunder

Release Date: April 8, 2009 [EBook #28536]

Language: English

Character set encoding: ISO-8859-1

*** START OF THIS PROJECT GUTENBERG EBOOK THE ASTRONOMY OF THE BIBLE ***

THE ASTRONOMY

OF THE BIBLE

AN ELEMENTARY COMMENTARY ON THE
ASTRONOMICAL REFERENCES
OF HOLY SCRIPTURE

BY

E. WALTER MAUNDER, F.R.A.S.

AUTHOR OF
'THE ROYAL OBSERVATORY, GREENWICH: ITS HISTORY AND WORK,'
AND 'ASTRONOMY WITHOUT A TELESCOPE'

PREFACE

Why should an astronomer write a commentary on the Bible?

Because commentators as a rule are not astronomers, and therefore either pass over the astronomical allusions of Scripture in silence, or else annotate them in a way which, from a scientific point of view, leaves much to be desired.

Astronomical allusions in the Bible, direct and indirect, are not few in number, and, in order to bring out their full significance, need to be treated astronomically. Astronomy further gives us the power of placing ourselves to some degree in the position of the patriarchs and prophets of old. We know that the same sun and moon, stars and planets, shine upon us as shone upon Abraham and Moses, David and Isaiah. We can, if we will, see the unchanging heavens with their eyes, and understand their attitude towards them.

It is worth while for us so to do. For the immense advances in science, made since the Canon of Holy Scripture was closed, and especially during the last three hundred years, may enable us to realize the significance of a most remarkable fact. Even in those early ages, [viii]when to all the nations surrounding Israel the heavenly bodies were objects for divination or idolatry, the attitude of the sacred writers toward them was perfect in its sanity and truth.

Astronomy has a yet further part to play in Biblical study. The dating of the several books of the Bible, and the relation of certain heathen mythologies to the Scripture narratives of the world's earliest ages, have received much attention of late years. Literary analysis has thrown much light on these subjects, but hitherto any evidence that astronomy could give has been almost wholly neglected; although, from the nature of the case, such evidence, so far as it is available, must be most decisive and exact.

I have endeavoured, in the present book, to make an astronomical commentary on the Bible, in a manner that shall be both clear and interesting to the general reader, dispensing as far as possible with astronomical technicalities, since the principles concerned are, for the most part, quite simple. I trust, also, that I have taken the first step in a new inquiry which promises to give results of no small importance.

E. Walter Maunder.

St.   John's,   London,   S.E.
January 1908.

CONTENTS

BOOK I

THE HEAVENLY BODIES

Chapter I. The Hebrew and Astronomy

- Modern Astronomy—Astronomy in the Classical Age—The Canon of Holy Scripture closed before the Classical Age—Character of the Scriptural References to the Heavenly Bodies—Tradition of Solomon's Eminence in Science—Attitude towards Nature of the Sacred Writers—Plan of the Book 3

CHAPTER I

THE HEBREW AND ASTRONOMY

Modern astronomy began a little more than three centuries ago with the invention of the telescope and Galileo's application of it to the study of the heavenly bodies. This new instrument at once revealed to him the mountains on the moon, the satellites of Jupiter, and the spots on the sun, and brought the celestial bodies under observation in a way that no one had dreamed of before. In our view to-day, the planets of the solar system are worlds; we can examine their surfaces and judge wherein they resemble or differ from our earth. To the ancients they were but points of light; to us they are vast bodies that we have been able to measure and to weigh. The telescope has enabled us also to penetrate deep into outer space; we have learnt of other systems besides that of our own sun and its dependents, many of them far more complex; clusters and clouds of stars have been [4]revealed to us, and mysterious nebulæ, which suggest by their forms that they are systems of suns in the making. More lately the invention of the spectroscope has informed us of the very elements which go to the composition of these numberless stars, and we can distinguish those which are in a similar condition to our sun from those differing from him. And photography has recorded for us objects too faint for mere sight to detect, even when aided by the most powerful telescope; too detailed and intricate for the most skilful hand to depict.

Galileo's friend and contemporary, Kepler, laid the foundations of another department of modern astronomy at about the same time. He studied the apparent movements of the planets until they yielded him their secret so far that he was able to express them in three simple laws, laws which, two generations later, Sir Isaac Newton demonstrated to be the outcome of one grand and simple law of universal range, the law of gravitation. Upon this law the marvellous mathematical conquests of astronomy have been based.

All these wonderful results have been attained by the free exercise of men's mental abilities, and it cannot be imagined that God would have intervened to hamper their growth in intellectual power by revealing to men facts and methods which it was within their own ability to discover for themselves. Men's mental powers have developed by their exercise; they would have been stunted had men been led to look to revelation rather than to diligent effort for the satisfaction of their curiosity. We therefore do not find any reference in the Bible to that which[5]modern astronomy has taught us. Yet it may be noted that some expressions, appropriate at any time, have become much more appropriate, much more forcible, in the light of our present-day knowledge.

The age of astronomy which preceded the Modern, and may be called the Classical age, was almost as sharply defined in its beginning as its successor. It lasted about two thousand years, and began with the investigations into the movements of the planets made by some of the early

62

Greek mathematicians. Classical, like Modern astronomy, had its two sides,—the instrumental and the mathematical. On the instrumental side was the invention of graduated instruments for the determination of the positions of the heavenly bodies; on the mathematical, the development of geometry and trigonometry for the interpretation of those positions when thus determined. Amongst the great names of this period are those of Eudoxus of Knidus (B.C. 408-355), and Hipparchus of Bithynia, who lived rather more than two centuries later. Under its first leaders astronomy in the Classical age began to advance rapidly, but it soon experienced a deadly blight. Men were not content to observe the heavenly bodies for what they were; they endeavoured to make them the sources of divination. The great school of Alexandria (founded about 300 B.C.), the headquarters of astronomy, became invaded by the spirit of astrology, the bastard science which has always tried—parasite-like—to suck its life from astronomy. Thus from the days of Claudius Ptolemy to the end of the Middle Ages the growth of astronomy was arrested, and it bore but little fruit.

[6]It will be noticed that the Classical age did not commence until about the time of the completion of the last books of the Old Testament; so we do not find any reference in Holy Scripture to the astronomical achievements of that period, amongst which the first attempts to explain the apparent motions of sun, moon, stars, and planets were the most considerable.

We have a complete history of astronomy in the Modern and Classical periods, but there was an earlier astronomy, not inconsiderable in amount, of which no history is preserved. For when Eudoxus commenced his labours, the length of the year had already been determined, the equinoxes and solstices had been recognized, the ecliptic, the celestial equator, and the poles of both great circles were known, and the five principal planets were familiar objects. This Early astronomy must have had its history, its stages of development, but we can only with difficulty trace them out. It cannot have sprung into existence full-grown any more than the other sciences; it must have started from zero, and men must have slowly fought their way from one observation to another, with gradually widening conceptions, before they could bring it even to that stage of development in which it was when the observers of the Museum of Alexandria began their work.

The books of the Old Testament were written at different times during the progress of this Early age of astronomy. We should therefore naturally expect to find the astronomical allusions written from the standpoint of such scientific knowledge as had then been acquired. We cannot for a moment expect that any [7]supernatural revelation of purely material facts would be imparted to the writers of sacred books, two or three thousand years before the progress of science had brought those facts to light, and we ought not to be surprised if expressions are occasionally used which we should not ourselves use to-day, if we were writing about the phenomena of nature from a technical point of view. It must further be borne in mind that the astronomical references are not numerous, that they occur mostly in poetic imagery, and that Holy Scripture was not intended to give an account of the scientific achievements, if any, of the Hebrews of old. Its purpose was wholly different: it was religious, not scientific; it was meant to give spiritual, not intellectual enlightenment.

An exceedingly valuable and interesting work has recently been brought out by the most eminent of living Italian astronomers, Prof. G. V. Schiaparelli, on this subject of "Astronomy in the Old Testament," to which work I should like here to acknowledge my indebtedness. Yet I feel that the avowed object of his book,[7.11]—to "discover what ideas the ancient Jewish sages held regarding the structure of the universe, what observations they made of the stars, and how far they made use of them for the measurement and division of time"—is open to this criticism,—that sufficient material for carrying it out is not within our reach. If we were to accept implicitly the argument from the silence of Scripture, we should conclude that the Hebrews—though their calendar was essentially a lunar one, based upon the [8]actual observation of the new moon—had never noticed that the moon changed its apparent form as the month wore on, for there is no mention in the Bible of the lunar phases.

The references to the heavenly bodies in Scripture are not numerous, and deal with them either as time-measurers or as subjects for devout allusion, poetic simile, or symbolic use. But there is one characteristic of all these references to the phenomena of Nature, that may not be ignored. None of the ancients ever approached the great Hebrew writers in spiritual elevation; none equalled them in poetic sublimity; and few, if any, surpassed them in keenness of observation, or in quick sympathy with every work of the Creator.

These characteristics imply a natural fitness of the Hebrews for successful scientific work, and we should have a right to believe that under propitious circumstances they would have shown a pre-eminence in the field of physical research as striking as is the superiority of their religious conceptions over those of the surrounding nations. We cannot, of course, conceive of the average Jew as an Isaiah, any more than we can conceive of the average Englishman as a Shakespeare, yet the one man, like the other, is an index of the advancement and capacity of his race; nor could Isaiah's writings have been preserved, more than those of Shakespeare, without a true appreciation of them on the part of many of his countrymen.

But the necessary conditions for any great scientific development were lacking to Israel. A small nation, [9]planted between powerful and aggressive empires, their history was for the most part the record of a struggle for bare existence; and after three or four centuries of the unequal conflict, first the one and then the other of the two sister kingdoms was overwhelmed. There was but little opportunity during these years of storm and stress for men to indulge in any curious searchings into the secrets of nature.

Once only was there a long interval of prosperity and peace; viz. from the time that David had consolidated the kingdom to the time when it suffered disruption under his grandson, Rehoboam; and it is significant that tradition has ascribed to Solomon and to his times just such a scientific activity as the ability and temperament of the Hebrew race would lead us to expect it to display when the conditions should be favourable for it.

Thus, in the fourth chapter of the First Book of Kings, not only are the attainments of Solomon himself described, but other men, contemporaries either of his father David or himself, are referred to, as distinguished in the same direction, though to a less degree.

"And God gave Solomon wisdom and understanding exceeding much, and largeness of heart, even as the sand that is on the seashore. And Solomon's wisdom excelled the wisdom of all the children of the east country, and all the wisdom of Egypt. For he was wiser than all men; than Ethan the Ezrahite, and Heman, and Chalcol, and Darda, the sons of Mahol: and his fame was in all nations round about. And he spake three thousand proverbs: and his songs were a thousand and five. And he spake of trees, from the cedar-tree that is in Lebanon even unto the hyssop that springeth out of the wall: he spake also of [10]beasts, and of fowl, and of creeping things, and of fishes. And there came of all people to hear the wisdom of Solomon, from all kings of the earth, which had heard of his wisdom."

The tradition of his great eminence in scientific research is also preserved in the words put into his mouth in the Book of the Wisdom of Solomon, now included in the Apocrypha.

"For" (God) "Himself gave me an unerring knowledge of the things that are, to know the constitution of the world, and the operation of the elements; the beginning and end and middle of times, the alternations of the solstices and the changes of seasons, the circuits of years and the positions" (*margin*, constellations) "of stars; the natures of living creatures and the ragings of wild beasts, the violences of winds and the thoughts of men, the diversities of plants and the virtues of roots: all things that are either secret or manifest I learned, for she that is the artificer of all things taught me, even Wisdom."

Two great names have impressed themselves upon every part of the East:—the one, that of Solomon the son of David, as the master of every secret source of knowledge; and the other that of Alexander the Great, as the mightiest of conquerors. It is not unreasonable to believe that the traditions respecting the first have been founded upon as real a basis of actual achievement as those respecting the second.

But to such scientific achievements we have no express allusion in Scripture, other than is afforded us by the two quotations just made. Natural objects, natural phenomena are not referred to for their own sake. Every [11]thought leads up to God or to man's relation to Him. Nature, as a whole and in its every aspect and detail, is the handiwork of Jehovah: that is the truth which the heavens are always declaring;—and it is His power, His wisdom, and His goodness to man which it is sought to illustrate, when the beauty or wonder of natural objects is described.

"When I consider Thy heavens, the work of Thy fingers,The moon and the stars, which Thou hast ordained;What is man, that Thou art mindful of him?And the son of man, that Thou visitest him?"

The first purpose, therefore, of the following study of the astronomy of the Bible is,—not to reconstruct the astronomy of the Hebrews, a task for which the material is manifestly incomplete,—but to examine such astronomical allusions as occur with respect to their appropriateness to the lesson which the writer desired to teach. Following this, it will be of interest to examine what connection can be traced between the Old Testament Scriptures and the Constellations; the arrangement of the stars into constellations having been the chief astronomical work effected during the centuries when those Scriptures were severally composed. The use made of the heavenly bodies as time-measurers amongst the Hebrews will form a third division of the subject; whilst there are two or three incidents in the history of Israel which appear to call for examination from an astronomical point of view, and may suitably be treated in a fourth and concluding section.

This page blank on purpose

You may doodle here

Week 12 Review Questions

From Class and Signs & Seasons, Epilogue, the Calendar, starting on p.167

1. What does Genesis 1:14 say?
    a. And God set them in the expanse of the heavens to give light on the earth,
    b. The heavens declare the glory of God, and the sky above proclaims his handiwork.
    c. And God said, "Let there be lights in the expanse of the heavens to separate the day from the night. And let them be for signs and for seasons, and for days and years,
    d. When I look at your heavens, the work of your fingers, the moon and the stars, which you have set in place.

2. What is the period of a lunar cycle?
    a. 25.5 days   b. 29.5 days   c. Exactly 30 days   d. 365¼ days

3. A lunar calendar of 12 lunar cycles (months) would be how long?
    a. 354   b. 365   c. 384   d. 1000

4. There are "intercalary" months and "intercalary" days; what is intercalary?
    a. Latin for "to call among" which is adding months or days into the calendar.
    b. Latin for "to call among" which is subtracting months or days into the calendar.
    c. Latin for "start over" which is clearing out the calendar and starting a new year.
    d. Egyptian for "you must be kidding" which is abandoning the lunar calendar system.

5. Who used the Luni-Solar Calendar?
    a. Egyptians, Romans & Greeks   b. Babylonians, Muslims & Hebrews
    c. Babylonians, Egyptians & Hebrews   d. Babylonians & Hebrews

6. How many years was the Luni-Solar Calendar cycle?
    a. 4   b. 12   c. 19   d. 7

7. T/F. Islamic months are not in the same season year after year.

8. What star did the ancient Egyptians take very seriously?
    a. Polaris   b. Sirius   c. Betelgeuse   d. Algol

9. What kind of calendar system did the ancient Egyptians use?
    a. The Julian calendar   b. A basic solar calendar of 365.25 days
    c. The Gregorian calendar   d. The Luni-Solar Calendar

10. T/F. Julius Caesar visited Solomon and adopted the Hebrew calendar in 405 BC.

11. T/F. In the book of Exodus, Moses set up a lunar calendar which is still used in Israel today.

12. Who did Julius Caesar fashion his calendar from?
    a. The Egyptians   b. The Greeks
    c. The Babylonians   d. The Hebrews

13. T/F. Sirius is our brightest star. (Apparent)

14. How many intercalary months are in the Julian calendar?
    a. One every four years   b. One every three years
    c. 12 in a 19 year period   d. Zero

15. How many intercalary days are in the Julian calendar?
    a. One every other year   b. One every fourth year
    c. Six to start off in 54BC then zero after that   d. Zero

16. What was wrong with the Julian calendar?
    a. It was about 11 minutes off which adds up after awhile
    b. It was about 11 hours off which adds up after awhile
    c. It was about 11 seconds off which adds up after awhile
    d. It was Roman and the Catholics don't like Rome

17. Concerning the calendar, what was the early Church obsessed with getting right?
    a. The exact date of Christ birth
    b. An accurate, reliable date for celebrating Easter
    c. Knowing when the Summer Solstice began
    d. The number of missing days in the Egyptian calendar

18. When was the first adoption of the Gregorian Calendar?
    a. 1752   b. 1918   c. 1582   d. 54 BC

19. What was the Gregorian calendar's first adjustment?
    a. Omitting the month of October in 1582
    b. Omitting 10 days in October of 1582
    c. Omitting 11 days in October of 1752
    d. Adding February 29 to the calendar every four years

20. When is the Vernal Equinox?
    a. When the Moon and the Sun are in Aries
    b. When Sirius becomes visible before sunrise
    c. When the Sun's journey intersects the celestial equator in spring.
    d. When the Moon's journey crosses the celestial equator in spring.

21. When did the Church definitively settle the criteria for determining Easter?
    a. When Pope Gregory initiated the Gregorian calendar
    b. At the Council of Nicaea in A.D.325
    c. When Julius Ceaser reformed the calendar in 54BC
    d. When Napoleon was defeated at Waterloo

22. How is the date for Easter determined?
    a. The first Sunday following the first New Moon after the Vernal Equinox
    b. The first Sunday following the first Full Moon after the Vernal Equinox
    c. The first Sunday following the first Full Moon after the Spring Solstice
    d. The first Monday following the first Full Moon after the Vernal Equinox

23. How does the Gregorian calendar prevent the date for the Vernal Equinox from changing over many centuries?
    a. It stops the Sun for 12 hours every 500 years.
    b. It adds a February 30th every 400 years.
    c. It skips having a leap year on 3 of 4 century years.
    d. It skips all leap years ending in 00.

24. Does the word "Easter" come from a non-Christian tradition?
    a. No   b. Probably

25. On page 179, JR mentions the Venerable Bede. Do a web or library search of him and provide five important points about him. As much as possible do your search on things related to astronomy. Use more than one source.

_____

_____

_____

_____

_____

Week 12 Activity

Sun Azimuth & Elevation Part II

Two months ago (week 4) you determined the Sun's azimuth and elevation. Recall for azimuth, we're interested in where does the sun rise or set. You used a directional compass. For the elevation, you went out at noon with a stick to ascertain how high the noon sun was.

Now let's see if we can notice a difference two months later. Fill in the chart below.
The website is: ***http://www.timeanddate.com/sun/usa/syracuse*** remember to put in your nearest city.

	W4 actual	W4 true (from website)	W12 actual	W12 true (from website)
Azimuth (sunrise or sunset)				
Noon Elevation				

1. How close were your measurements to the real thing? _____

_____

2. What did the sun do in those two months, be precise? _____

_____

_____

Week 13 Review Questions

Sun Azimuth & Elevation Review (see video)

1. What is the connection between the tilt of the earth and the tropic of cancer and tropic of Capricorn?
    a. There is no connection; they have nothing to do with each other
    b. The tilt of the earth is 30^0 so each of the tropics are 15^0.
    c. The tilt of the earth causes the tropics to move every 26,000 years
    d. The tilt of the earth is 23.5^0, and therefore the latitude of the tropics are 23.5^0 north and south respectively.

2. What is the connection between the tropics and the zodiac signs?
    a. There is no connection; they have nothing to do with each other
    b. When the tropics were first named the sun was in Cancer on vernal equinox and in Capricorn on autumn equinox.
    c. When the tropics were first named the moon was in Cancer on vernal equinox and in Capricorn on autumn equinox.
    d. The couple who named the tropics were born under those two signs.

3. What is the apparent tracking of the sun on Vernal Equinox?
    a. Over the equator
    c. Over the tropic of Cancer
    d. Over the tropic of Capricorn
    e. Along the 10^0 north latitude line

4. What is the apparent tracking of the sun on the northern hemisphere's Summer Solstice?
    a. Over the equator
    c. Over the tropic of Cancer
    d. Over the tropic of Capricorn
    e. Along the 20^0 north latitude line

5. (Use the Farmers' Almanac for this one.) On the 51st week, what is the length of day difference between the northern states and southern states?
    a. The length of day is the same for both locations
    b. 29 minutes
    c. 28 minutes
    d. 1 hour and 3 minutes

From Class

6. Provide three reasons why it is important to study the constellations? (3)
    a. _____

    b. _____

    c. _____

7. T/F. The pictures in the sky (constellations) come from a simple "connect the dots" type arrangement of the stars.

8. How many constellations are there today and how many did Ptolemy catalog?
    a. 90 & 45   b. 88 & 48   c. 88 & 87   d. 50 & 48

9. What are the constellations called that lie along the ecliptic?
    a. The Solar Constellations   b. The Astrology Constellations
    c. The Zodiac   d. The ecliptic constellations

10. Matching (3)

137 AD	Eudoxus
240 BC	Hesiod and Homer
400 BC	Aratus of Soli
800-600 BC	Babylonian Boundary Stones
1100 BC	Claudius Ptolemy

11. Who did the Apostle Paul quote in Acts 17?
    a. Aratus of Soli   b. Claudius Ptolemy
    c. Eudoxus   d. Homer

12. In ancient times, why were there fewer constellations? (2)

_____

13. Where does Maunder believe the original constellations could NOT have originated?
    a. Egypt   b. Babylon   c. India   d. All the above

14. According to Maunder, when did the constellations come into existence?
    a. During the late Greek period, about 300 BC
    b. During the first Egyptian Dynasty, about 1800 BC
    c. Shortly after the New Testament was completed, about 70 AD
    d. 3,000 to 2,700 BC

15. What part of the Biblical account of Noah and the flood is **_NOT_** depicted in the constellations?
    a. The dove   b. The ark or ship   c. The raven   d. The Alter

16. Match the constellation with their placement in the sky.

North - where the constellations are visible all night.	Serpens the Serpent
South - Looking just below the equator	Scorpius the Scorpion
The meridian at midnight at the time of the Spring Equinox	Draco the Dragon
Where the meridian, the celestial equator and the ecliptic intersect	Hydra the water serpent

17. T/F. The promise given in Genesis 3:15 appear to be depicted in the sky.

18. What do cherubim's looks like? (Name the four likenesses)

_____

From our zodiac memorization project

19. Match the zodiac with the season. (From a nighttime viewing perspective)

Summer	Gemini
Fall	Virgo
Winter	Sagittarius
Spring	Pisces

From *The Astronomy of the Bib*le, Chapter II (pp.76-82)

20.1. The 5 W's. (3)

Where did M. go? _____

When did he go there? _____

What did he see? _____

Why did he go to see it? _____

Who else did the same thing? _____

21.2. Besides scientist, who else was present for the event? Why? (2) _____

_____

22.3. Since the sun and moon are so critical to life, what is understandably the next logical step concerning them? (3)

_____

_____

23.4. Do you think the 'heathens' participating in the eclipse also had telescopes and cameras handy? Yes   No

24.5. T/F. The very concept of science requires there be one universal law, and that law is called the Law of Causality (2)

25.6. If the law of causality **is not** universal, what does M. say about scientific observation? (2)

_____

26.7. If the law of causality **IS** universal, what does scientific observation do for us?

_____

27.8. Which statement best summarizes M's point in section Eight? (3)
    a. The heathens of old are different that the heathens today because they have modern science to prove their point.
    b. The ancient Hebrews belief in one God doesn't have anything to do with scientific observations.
    c. The first words of the Bible changed everything; it opened the door for science instead of silly superstition and gave us the law of causality because there is one God.
    d. The reason the Jews have contributed so much to science is they are guided by the opening words of Genesis.

28.8. (paraphrased) The first words of Genesis may be called the charter of all the _____ _____. (2 words)

29.9. Provide me at least three things that M. says science _**cannot**_ do and then tell me M's main point of this paragraph. (4)

_____

_____

_____

_____

30.10. List the three things M. says men cannot find out for themselves. (2)

_____

_____

_____

31.11. T/F. Science will ultimately be able to prove the accuracy of Genesis chapter 1.

32.12. M. quotes Hebrews; what chapter and verse is it? _____ (2)

Week 13 Activity
Winter Items

Watch my Week 13 video. Capitalize on a clear night and find these 10 winter stars and asterisms.   10 points for each item.

Put your story in the dropbox; include date time, circumstances and any other pertinent facts.

1. Pleiades

2. Orion's Belt

3. Orion's Sword

4. Rigel

5. Betelgeuse

6. Capella

7. Castor

8. Pollux

9. Procyon

10 Sirius

The Astronomy of the Bible

E. Walter Maunder

CHAPTER II

THE CREATION

A few years ago a great eclipse of the sun, seen as total along a broad belt of country right across India, drew thither astronomers from the very ends of the earth. Not only did many English observers travel thither, but the United States of America in the far west, and Japan in the far east sent their contingents, and the entire length of country covered by the path of the shadow was dotted with the temporary observatories set up by the men of science.

It was a wonderful sight that was vouchsafed to these travellers in pursuit of knowledge. In a sky of unbroken purity, undimmed even for a moment by haze or cloud, there shone down the fierce Indian sun. Gradually a dark mysterious circle invaded its lower edge, and covered its brightness; coolness replaced the burning heat; slowly the dark covering crept on; slowly the sunlight diminished until at length the whole of the sun's disc was hidden. Then in a moment a wonderful starlike form flashed out, a noble form of glowing silver light on the deep purple-coloured sky.

There was, however, no time for the astronomers to devote to admiration of the beauty of the scene, or indulgence in rhapsodies. Two short minutes alone were allotted them to note all that was happening, to take all their photographs, to ask all the questions, and obtain all the answers for which this strange veiling of the sun, and still stranger unveiling of his halo-like surroundings, gave opportunity. It was two minutes of intensest strain, of hurried though orderly work; and then a sudden rush of sunlight put an end to all. The mysterious vision had withdrawn itself; the colour rushed back to the landscape, so corpse-like whilst in the shadow; the black veil slid rapidly from off the sun; the heat returned to the air; the eclipse was over.

But the astronomers from distant lands were not the only people engaged in watching the eclipse. At their work, they could hear the sound of a great multitude, a sound of weeping and wailing, a people dismayed at the distress of their god.

It was so at every point along the shadow track, but especially where that track met the course of the sacred river. Along a hundred roads the pilgrims had poured in unceasing streams towards Holy Mother Gunga; towards Benares, the sacred city; towards Buxar, where the eclipse was central at the river bank. It is always meritorious—so the Hindoo holds—to bathe in that sacred river, but such a time as this, when the sun is in eclipse, is the most propitious moment of all for such lustration.

Could there be a greater contrast than that offered between the millions trembling and dismayed at the signs of heaven, and the little companies who had come for thousands of miles over land

and sea, rejoicing in the brief chance that was given them for learning a little more of the secrets of the wonders of Nature?

The contrast between the heathen and the scientists was in both their spiritual and their intellectual standpoint, and, as we shall see later, the intellectual contrast is a result of the spiritual. The heathen idea is that the orbs of heaven are divine, or at least that each expresses a divinity. This does not in itself seem an unnatural idea when we consider the great benefits that come to us through the instrumentality of the sun and moon. It is the sun that morning by morning rolls back the darkness, and brings light and warmth and returning life to men; it is the sun that rouses the earth after her winter sleep and quickens vegetation. It is the moon that has power over the great world of waters, whose pulse beats in some kind of mysterious obedience to her will.

Natural, then, has it been for men to go further, and to suppose that not only is power lodged in these, and in the other members of the heavenly host, but that it is living, intelligent, personal power; that these shining orbs are beings, or the manifestations of beings; exalted, mighty, immortal;—that they are gods.

But if these are gods, then it is sacrilegious, it is profane, to treat them as mere "things"; to observe them minutely in the microscope or telescope; to dissect them, as it were, in the spectroscope; to identify their elements in the laboratory; to be curious about their properties, influences, relations, and actions on each other.

And if these are gods, there are many gods, not One God. And if there are many gods, there are many laws, not one law. Thus scientific observations cannot be reconciled with polytheism, for scientific observations demand the assumption of one universal law. The wise king expressed this law thus:—

"The thing that hath been, it is that which shall be." The actual language of science, as expressed by Professor Thiele, a leading Continental astronomer, states that—

"Everything that exists, and everything that happens, exists or happens as a necessary consequence of a previous state of things. If a state of things is repeated in every detail, it must lead to exactly the same consequences. Any difference between the results of causes that are in part the same, must be explainable by some difference in the other part of the causes."[15:1]

The law stated in the above words has been called the Law of Causality. It "cannot be proved, but must be believed; in the same way as we believe the fundamental assumptions of religion, with which it is closely and intimately connected. The law of causality forces itself upon our belief. It may be denied in theory, but not in practice. Any person who denies it, will, if he is watchful enough, catch himself constantly asking himself, if no one else, why this has happened, and not that. But in that very question he bears witness to the law of causality. If we are consistently to deny the law of causality, we must repudiate all observation, and particularly all prediction based on past experience, as useless and misleading.

"If we could imagine for an instant that the same complete combination of causes could have a definite number of different consequences, however small that number might be, and that among these the occurrence of the actual consequence was, in the old sense of the word, accidental, no observation would ever be of any particular value."[16:1]

So long as men hold, as a practical faith, that the results which attend their efforts depend upon whether Jupiter is awake and active, or Neptune is taking an unfair advantage of his brother's sleep; upon whether Diana is bending her silver bow for the battle, or flying weeping and discomfited because Juno has boxed her ears—so long is it useless for them to make or consult observations.

But, as Professor Thiele goes on to say—

"If the law of causality is acknowledged to be an assumption which always holds good, then every observation gives us a revelation which, when correctly appraised and compared with others, teaches us the laws by which God rules the world."

By what means have the modern scientists arrived at a position so different from that of the heathen? It cannot have been by any process of natural evolution that the intellectual standpoint which has made scientific observation possible should be derived from the spiritual standpoint of polytheism which rendered all scientific observation not only profane but useless.

In the old days the heathen in general regarded the heavenly host and the heavenly bodies as the heathen do to-day. But by one nation, the Hebrews, the truth that—

"In the beginning God created the heaven and the earth"

was preserved in the first words of their Sacred Book. That nation declared—

"All the gods of the people are idols: but the Lord made the heavens."

For that same nation the watchword was—

Hear, O Israel: the Lord our God is one Lord."

From these words the Hebrews not only learned a great spiritual truth, but derived intellectual freedom. For by these words they were taught that all the host of heaven and of earth were created things—merely "things," not divinities—and not only that, but that the Creator was One God, not many gods; that there was but one law-giver; and that therefore there could be no conflict of laws. These first words of Genesis, then, may be called the charter of all the physical sciences, for by them is conferred freedom from all the bonds of unscientific superstition, and by them also do men know that consistent law holds throughout the whole universe. It is the intellectual freedom of the Hebrew that the scientist of to-day inherits. He may not indeed be able to rise to the spiritual standpoint of the Hebrew, and consciously acknowledge that—

"Thou, even Thou, art Lord alone; Thou hast made heaven, the heaven of heavens, with all their host, the earth, and all things that are therein, the seas, and all that is therein, and Thou preservest them all; and the host of heaven worshippeth Thee."

But he must at least unconsciously assent to it, for it is on the first great fundamental assumption of religion as stated in the first words of Genesis, that the fundamental assumption of all his scientific reasoning depends.

Scientific reasoning and scientific observation can only hold good so long and in so far as the Law of Causality holds good. We must assume a pre-existing state of affairs which has given rise to the observed effect; we must assume that this observed effect is itself antecedent to a subsequent state of affairs. Science therefore cannot go back to the absolute beginnings of things, or forward to the absolute ends of things. It cannot reason about the way matter and energy came into existence, or how they might cease to exist; it cannot reason about time or space, as such, but only in the relations of these to phenomena that can be observed. It does not deal with things themselves, but only with the relations between things. Science indeed can only consider the universe as a great machine which is in "going order," and it concerns itself with the relations which some parts of the machine bear to other parts, and with the laws and manner of the "going" of the machine in those parts. The relations of the various parts, one to the other, and the way in which they work together, may afford some idea of the design and purpose of the machine, but it can give no information as to how the material of which it is composed came into existence, nor as to the method by which it was originally constructed. Once started, the machine comes under the scrutiny of science, but the actual starting lies outside its scope.

Men therefore cannot find out for themselves how the worlds were originally made, how the worlds were first moved, or how the spirit of man was first formed within him; and this, not merely because these beginnings of things were of necessity outside his experience, but also because beginnings, as such, must lie outside the law by which he reasons.

By no process of research, therefore, could man find out for himself the facts that are stated in the first chapter of Genesis. They must have been revealed. Science cannot inquire into them for the purpose of checking their accuracy; it must accept them, as it accepts the fundamental law that governs its own working, without the possibility of proof.

And this is what has been revealed to man:—that the heaven and the earth were not self-existent from all eternity, but were in their first beginning created by God. As the writer of the Epistle to the Hebrews expresses it: "Through faith we understand that the worlds were framed by the word of God, so that things which are seen were not made of things which do appear." And a further fact was revealed that man could not have found out for himself; viz. that this creation was made and finished in six Divine actings, comprised in what the narrative denominates "days." It has not been revealed whether the duration of these "days" can be expressed in any astronomical units of time.

 Since under these conditions science can afford no information, it is not to be wondered at that the hypotheses that have been framed from time to time to "explain" the first chapter of Genesis, or to express it in scientific terms, are not wholly satisfactory. At one time the chapter was interpreted to mean that the entire universe was called into existence about 6,000 years ago, in six days of twenty-four hours each. Later it was recognized that both geology and astronomy seemed to indicate the existence of matter for untold millions of years instead of some six thousand. It was then pointed out that, so far as the narrative was concerned, there might have been a period of almost unlimited duration between its first verse and its fourth; and it was suggested that the six days of creation were six days of twenty-four hours each, in which, after some great cataclysm, 6,000 years ago, the face of the earth was renewed and replenished for the habitation of man, the preceding geological ages being left entirely unnoticed. Some writers have confined the cataclysm and renewal to a small portion of the earth's surface—to "Eden," and its neighbourhood. Other commentators have laid stress on the truth revealed in Scripture that "one day is with the Lord as a thousand years, and a thousand years as one day," and have urged the argument that the six days of creation were really vast periods of time, during which the earth's geological changes and the evolution of its varied forms of life were running their course. Others, again, have urged that the six days of creation were six literal days, but instead of being consecutive were separated by long ages. And yet again, as no man was present during the creation period, it has been suggested that the Divine revelation of it was given to Moses or some other inspired prophet in six successive visions or dreams, which constituted the "six days" in which the chief facts of creation were set forth.

All such hypotheses are based on the assumption that the opening chapters of Genesis are intended to reveal to man certain physical details in the material history of this planet; to be in fact a little compendium of the geological and zoological history of the world, and so a suitable introduction to the history of the early days of mankind which followed it.

It is surely more reasonable to conclude that there was no purpose whatever of teaching us anything about the physical relationships of land and sea, of tree and plant, of bird and fish; it seems, indeed, scarcely conceivable that it should have been the Divine intention so to supply the ages with a condensed manual of the physical sciences. What useful purpose could it have served? What man would have been the wiser or better for it? Who could have understood it until the time when men, by their own intellectual strivings, had attained sufficient knowledge of their physical surroundings to do without such a revelation at all?

But although the opening chapters of Genesis were not designed to teach the Hebrew certain physical facts of nature, they gave him the knowledge that he might lawfully study nature. For he learnt from them that nature has no power nor vitality of its own; that sun, and sea, and cloud, and wind are not separate deities, nor the expression of deities that they are but "things," however glorious and admirable; that they are the handiwork of God; and—

"The works of the Lord are great, Sought out of all them that have pleasure therein. His work is honour and majesty; And His righteousness endureth for ever. He hath made His wonderful works to be remembered."

What, then, is the significance of the detailed account given us of the works effected on the successive days of creation? Why are we told that light was made on the first day, the firmament on the second, dry land on the third, and so on? Probably for two reasons. First, that the rehearsal, as in a catalogue, of the leading classes of natural objects, might give definiteness and precision to the teaching that each and all were creatures, things made by the word of God. The bald statement that the heaven and the earth were made by God might still have left room for the imagination that the powers of nature were co-eternal with God, or were at least subordinate divinities; or that other powers than God had worked up into the present order the materials He had created. The detailed account makes it clear that not only was the universe in general created by God, but that there was no part of it that was not fashioned by Him.

The next purpose was to set a seal of sanctity upon the Sabbath. In the second chapter of Genesis we read—

"On the seventh day God ended His work which He had made; and He rested on the seventh day from all His work which He had made. And God blessed the seventh day, and sanctified it: because that in it He had rested from all His work which God created and made."

In this we get the institution of the week, the first ordinance imposed by God upon man. For in the fourth of the Ten Commandments which God gave through Moses, it is said—

The seventh day is the sabbath of the Lord thy God: in it thou shalt not do any work. . . . For in six days the Lord made heaven and earth, the sea, and all that in them is, and rested the seventh day: wherefore the Lord blessed the sabbath day, and hallowed it."

And again, when the tabernacle was being builded, it was commanded—

"The children of Israel shall keep the sabbath, to observe the sabbath throughout their generations, for a perpetual covenant. It is a sign between Me and the children of Israel for ever: for in six days the Lord made heaven and earth, and on the seventh day He rested, and was refreshed."

God made the sun, moon, and stars, and appointed them "for signs, and for seasons, and for days, and years." The sun marks out the days; the moon by her changes makes the months; the sun and the stars mark out the seasons and the years. These were divisions of time which man would naturally adopt. But there is not an exact number of days in the month, nor an exact number of days or months in the year. Still less does the period of seven days fit precisely into month or season or year; the week is marked out by no phase of the moon, by no fixed relation between the sun, the moon, or the stars. It is not a division of time that man would naturally adopt for himself; it runs across all the natural divisions of time.

What are the six days of creative work, and the seventh day—the Sabbath—of creative rest? They are not days of man, they are days of God; and our days of work and rest, our week with its Sabbath, can only be the figure and shadow of that week of God; something by which we may gain some faint apprehension of its realities, not that by which we can comprehend and measure it.

Our week, therefore, is God's own direct appointment to us; and His revelation that He fulfilled the work of creation in six acts or stages, dignifies and exalts the toil of the labouring man, with his six days of effort and one of rest, into an emblem of the creative work of God.

Week 14 Review Questions

From Class

1. Three parts to this question (3)
    a. Name at least two of the constellations in this picture

    _____

    b. What is happening here? _____

    _____

    c. What Bible verse tells a similar story?

    _____

2. What is the constellation Virgo depicting?
        a. An angel   b. Farming in bare feet
        c. A maiden with seeds   d. Dancing in folk dress

3. What might the four constellations linked to the ancient astronomical timekeepers (2 solstices & 2 equinoxes) be associated with?
        a. Joseph's dream about his brothers'   b. The Cherubim guarding Eden
        c. The Golden Calf   d. Revelation

4. Jewish tradition has the constellation _____ as Nimrod, the mighty man in Gen 10.

5. T/F. Joseph's dream in Genesis 37 was all about those 15 constellations south of the ecliptic.

6. The Tribe of Judah is associated with what constellation?
        a. Leo the Lion   b. Taurus the ox
        c. Aquarius the Water Bearer   d. Aquila the Eagle

7. The Tribe of Ephraim (His father was Joseph) is associated with what constellation?
        a. Leo the Lion   b. Taurus the ox
        c. Serpens the snake   d. Scorpius the scorpion

8. The Tribe of Dan is associated with what constellation?
        a. Leo the Lion   b. Taurus the ox
        c. Aquarius the Water Bearer   d. Aquila the Eagle

9. The Tribe of Reuben?
        a. Leo the Lion   b. Taurus the ox
        c. Aquarius the Water Bearer   d. Aquila the Eagle

10. After leaving Egypt and while Moses was up in the mountain receiving the Ten Commandments; who where they honoring when they fashioned the golden calf and why?
     a. Judah because his sign was the Lion and lions like calves
     b. Joseph because his sign was the Ox which really could have been a calf
     c. Dan because his sign was an Eagle; but the eagle was too hard to make from gold
     d. Eve because her sign was Virgo and Eve was the one who named the calf.

11. How is it decided what "age" we're in, or what is the first of the zodiac signs?
     a. The Sun at Summer Solstice   b. The Sun at Summer Equinox
     b. The Sun at Winter Solstice   d. The Sun at Vernal Equinox

12. What would be the correct sequence of Zodiac leaders from the time of its origination until now?
     a. Virgo, Taurus, Pisces   b. Taurus, Aries, Aquarius
     c. Gemini, Taurus, Aries   d. Taurus, Aries, Pisces

13. Can you sing with me; "This is the dawning of the age of _____."

From Week 13 Activity Assignment

14. What is the most prominent feature of Orion?
     a. His Sword   b. His Belt   c. His Helmet   d. His Hair

15. What are the two prominent stars in Gemini?
     a. Aldebaran & Castor   b. Pollux and Procyon
     c. Castor & Pollux   d. Castor & Capella

16. What constellation is Betelgeuse in?
     a. Taurus   b. Canis Major   c. Gemini   d. Orion

17. What constellation are the Pleiades in?
     a. Taurus   b. Canis Major   c. Gemini   d. Orion

From *The Astronomy of the Bible*, Book II. Chapter VI (pp.87-96)

18.1. Do you get M's point in the first two paragraphs? What does the analogy of England's rivers have to do with the Pleiades? (3)

_____

_____

_____

19.2. What pejorative word does M. use to describe the American Indian and Australian savages? (2)

     _____

20.2. What three star groupings have been universally acknowledged and named? (2)

_____

21.3. What Hebrew word does M. think is correctly translated into English as the Pleiades? What are the three Bible verses where it is found? (3)

_____

22.4. What sentence best summarizes section 4? (2)

     a. Hebrew astronomy words were lost during their captivity in Babylon, except _Kimah_.

     b. The Hebrews adopted the Babylonian terms for the constellations during their captivity.

     c. The Hebrew word Ash means the bear, which is the big dipper.

     d. The Old Testament translation of the Hebrew into Greek preserved for us the meaning of _Kimah_.

23.5. What is likely true about the word origin of Pleiades?

     a. Latin for the back of a bull

     b. Greek for hunting with many arrows

     c. French for "rock pigeons"

     d. Greek for "many" and also connected with "birds"

24.6. T/F. The Babylonians and Assyrians believed the seven stars of the Pleiades were planets and worshipped them.

25.7. List at least four other names for the Pleiades (2)

     1. _____

     2. _____

     3. _____

     4. _____

26.7. Which statement is true about the number of stars are in the Pleiades? (3)

     a. There are currently only six stars; but in the past there were seven.

     b. Ancient literature and the Bible consistently refer to seven.

     c. On a clear night with good eyes you can only make out five

     d. The Bible identifies seven which stand for the days of creation.

27.8. T/F. The brightest star in the Pleiades, Alcyone, is the center of the Milky Way.

28.9. I get M's point that a Bible commentator named Drach was way off base trying to link Moses with certain astronomical occurrences.   But I don't get the last sentence of this paragraph. He seems to be saying its' equally goofy to link Easter Sunday to spring equinox. It is linked. Are you as confused as me?

_____

29.10. T/F. Because the Pleiades came up in late autumn, it was associated with the rainy season or floods.

30.11. M. finishes this chapter by giving his commentary on Job 38:32. Feel free to read it. But I want you to read the entire chapter of Job 38 and then tell me how you think verse 32 fits into God's overall point. (4)

_____

_____

_____

Note: No Activity this week. Catch up on missed activities or finish up your Astronomy Club visit report.

CHAPTER VI

THE PLEIADES

The translators of the Bible, from time to time, find themselves in a difficulty as to the correct rendering of certain words in the original. This is especially the case with the names of plants and animals. Some sort of clue may be given by the context, as, for instance, if the region is mentioned in which a certain plant is found, or the use that is made of it; or, in the case of an animal, whether it is "clean" or "unclean," what are its habits, and with what other animals it is associated. But in the case of the few Scripture references to special groups of stars, we have no such help. We are in the position in which Macaulay's New Zealander might be, if, long after the English nation had been dispersed, and its language had ceased to be spoken amongst men, he were to find a book in which the rivers "Thames," "Trent," "Tyne," and "Tweed" were mentioned by name, but without the slightest indication of their locality. His attempt to fit these names to particular rivers would be little more than a guess —a guess the accuracy of which he would have no means for testing.

This is somewhat our position with regard to the four Hebrew names, *Kīmah*, *Kĕsīl*, *'Ayish*, and *Mazzaroth*; yet in each case there are some slight indications which have given a clue to the compilers of our Revised Version, and have, in all probability, guided them correctly.

The constellations are not all equally attractive. A few have drawn the attention of all men, however otherwise inattentive. North-American Indians and Australian savages have equally noted the flashing brilliancy of Orion, and the compact little swarm of the Pleiades. All northern nations recognize the seven bright stars of the Great Bear, and they are known by a score of familiar names. They are the "Plough," or "Charles's Wain" of Northern Europe; the "Seven Plough Oxen" of ancient Rome; the "Bier and Mourners" of the Arabs; the "Chariot," or "Waggon," of the old Chaldeans; the "Big Dipper" of the prosaic New England farmer. These three groups are just the three which we find mentioned in the earliest poetry of Greece. So Homer writes, in the Fifth Book of the *Odyssey*, that Ulysses —

> "There view'd the Pleiads, and the Northern Team,
> And Great Orion's more refulgent beam,
> To which, around the axle of the sky,
> The Bear, revolving, points his golden eye."

It seems natural to conclude that these constellations, the most striking, or at all events the most universally recognized, would be those mentioned in the Bible.

The passages in which the Hebrew word *Kīmah*, is used are the following—

(God) "maketh Arcturus, Orion, and Pleiades (*Kīmah*), and the chambers of the south" (Job ix. 9).

"Canst thou bind the sweet influences of Pleiades (*Kīmah*), or loose the bands of Orion?" (Job xxxviii. 31).

"Seek Him that maketh the seven stars (*Kīmah*) and Orion" (Amos v. 8).

In our Revised Version, *Kīmah* is rendered "Pleiades" in all three instances, and of course the translators of the Authorized Version meant the same group by the "seven stars" in their free rendering of the passage from Amos. The word *kīmah* signifies "a heap," or "a cluster," and would seem to be related to the Assyrian word *kimtu*, "family," from a root meaning to "tie," or "bind"; a family being a number of persons bound together by the very closest tie of relationship. If this be so we can have no doubt that our translators have rightly rendered the word. There is one cluster in the sky, and one alone, which appeals to the unaided sight as being distinctly and unmistakably a family of stars—the Pleiades.

The names *'Ash*, or *'Ayish, Kĕsīl*, and *Kīmah* are peculiar to the Hebrews, and are not, so far as we have any evidence at present, allied to names in use for any constellation amongst the Babylonians and Assyrians; they have, as yet, not been found on any cuneiform inscription. Amos, the herdsman of Tekoa, living in the eighth century b.c., two centuries before the Jews were carried into exile to Babylon, evidently knew well what the terms signified, and the writer of the Book of Job was no less aware of their signification. But the "Seventy," who translated the Hebrew Scriptures into Greek, were not at all clear as to the identification of these names of constellations; though they made their translation only two or three centuries after the Jews returned to Jerusalem under Ezra and Nehemiah, when oral tradition should have still supplied the meaning of such astronomical terms. Had these names been then known in Babylon, they could not have been unknown to the learned men of Alexandria in the second century before our era, since at that time there was a very direct scientific influence of the one city upon the other. This Hebrew astronomy was so far from being due to Babylonian influence and teaching, that, though known centuries before the exile, after the exile we find the knowledge of its technical terms was lost. On the other hand, *kīma* was the term used in all Syriac literature to denominate the Pleiades, and we accordingly find in the Peschitta, the ancient Syriac version of the Bible, made about the second century a.d., the term *kīma* retained throughout, but *kesil* and *'ayish* were reduced to their supposed Syriac equivalents.

Whatever uncertainty was felt as to the meaning of *kīmah* by the early translators, it is not now seriously disputed that the Pleiades is the group of stars in question.

The word *kīmah* means, as we have seen, "cluster" or "heap," so also the word *Pleiades*, which we use to-day, is probably derived from the Greek *Pleiones*, "many." Several Greek poets—Athenæus, Hesiod, Pindar, and Simonides—wrote the word *Peleiades*, i. e. "rock pigeons," considered as flying from the Hunter Orion; others made them the seven doves who carried ambrosia to the infant Zeus. D'Arcy Thompson says, "The Pleiad is in many languages associated with bird-names, . . . and I am inclined to take the bird on the bull's back in coins of Eretria, Dicæa, and Thurii for the associated constellation of the Pleiad"[217:1]—the Pleiades being situated on the shoulder of Taurus the Bull.

The Hyades were situated on the head of the Bull, and in the Euphrates region these two little groups of stars were termed together, *Mas-tab-ba-gal-gal-la*, the Great Twins of the ecliptic, as Castor and Pollux were the Twins of the zodiac. In one tablet *'Imina bi*, "the sevenfold one," and *Gut-dûa*, "the Bull-in-front," are mentioned side by side, thus agreeing well with their interpretation of "Pleiades and Hyades." The Semitic name for the Pleiades was also *Têmennu*; and these groups of stars, worshipped as gods by the Babylonians, may possibly have been the *Gad* and *Meni*, "that troop," and "that number," referred to by the prophet Isaiah (lxv. 11).

On many Babylonian cylinder seals there are engraved seven small discs, in addition to other astronomical symbols. These seven small stellar discs are almost invariably arranged in the form :::' or :::· much as we should now-a-days plot the cluster of the Pleiades when mapping on a small scale the constellations round the Bull. It is evident that these seven little stellar discs do not mean the "seven planets," for in many cases the astronomical symbols which accompany them include both those of the sun and moon. It is most probable that they signify the Pleiades, or perhaps alternatively the Hyades.

Possibly, reference is made to the worship of the Pleiades when the king of Assyria, in the seventh century b.c., brought men from Babylon and other regions to inhabit the depopulated cities of Samaria, "and the men of Babylon made Succoth-benoth." The Rabbis are said to have rendered this by the "booths of the Maidens," or the "tents of the Daughters,"— the Pleiades being the maidens in question.

Generally they are the Seven Sisters. Hesiod calls them the Seven Virgins, and the Virgin Stars. The names given to the individual stars are those of the seven daughters of Atlas and Pleione; thus Milton terms them the Seven Atlantic Sisters.

As we have seen (p. 189), the device associated expressly with Joseph is the Bull, and Jacob's blessing to his son has been sometimes rendered—

"Joseph is a fruitful bough, even a fruitful bough by a well; *the daughters walk upon the bull.*"

That is, "the Seven Sisters," the Pleiades, are on the shoulder of Taurus.

Aratus wrote of the number of the Pleiades—

"Seven paths aloft men say they take,
Yet six alone are viewed by mortal eyes.
From Zeus' abode no star unknown is lost,
Since first from birth we heard, but thus the tale is told."

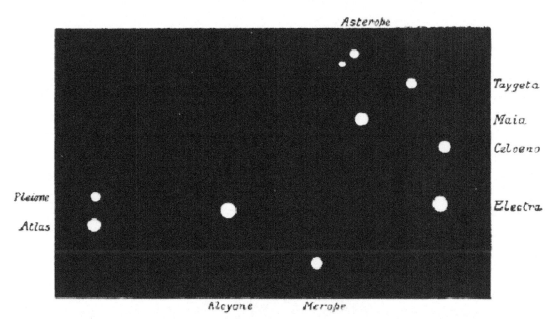

STARS OF THE PLEIADES. ToList

Euripides speaks of these "seven paths," and Eratosthenes calls them "the seven-starred Pleiad," although he describes one as "All-Invisible." There is a surprisingly universal tradition that they "were seven who now are six." We find it not only in ancient Greece and Italy, but also among the black fellows of Australia, the Malays of Borneo, and the negroes of the Gold Coast. There must be some reason to account for this widespread tradition. Some of the stars are known to be slightly variable, and one of the fainter stars in the cluster may have shone more brightly in olden time;—the gaseous spectrum of Pleione renders it credible that this star may once have had great brilliancy. Alcyone, now the brightest star in the cluster, was not mentioned by Ptolemy among the four brightest Pleiads of his day. The six now visible to ordinary sight are Alcyone, Electra, Atlas, Maia, Merope and Taygeta. Celoeno is the next in brightness, and the present candidate for the seventh place. By good sight, several more may be made out: thus Maestlin, the tutor of Kepler, mapped eleven before the invention of the telescope, and in our own day Carrington and Denning have counted fourteen with the naked eye.

In clear mountain atmosphere more than seven would be seen by any keen-sighted observer. Usually six stars may be made out with the naked eye in both the Pleiades and the Hyades, or, if more than six, then several more; though with both groups the number of "seven" has always been associated.

In the New Testament we find the "Seven Stars" also mentioned. In the first chapter of the Revelation, the Apostle St. John says that he "saw seven golden candlesticks; and in the midst of the seven candlesticks one like unto the Son of Man, . . . and He had in His right hand seven stars." Later in the same chapter it is explained that "the seven stars are the angels of the seven churches; and the seven candlesticks which thou sawest are the seven churches." The seven stars in a single compact cluster thus stand for the Church in its many diversities and its essential unity.

This beautiful little constellation has become associated with a foolish fable. When it was first found that not only did the planets move round the sun in orbits, but that the sun itself also was travelling rapidly through space, a German astronomer, Mädler, hazarded the suggestion that the centre of the sun's motion lay in the Pleiades. It was soon evident that there was no sufficient ground for this suggestion, and that many clearly established facts were inconsistent with it. Nevertheless the idea caught hold of the popular mind, and it has acquired an amazing vogue. Non-astronomical writers have asserted that Alcyone, the brightest Pleiad, is the centre of the entire universe; some have even been sufficiently irreverent to declare that it is the seat of heaven, the throne of God. A popular London divine, having noticed a bright ring round Alcyone on a photograph of the group, took that halo, which every photographer would at once recognize as a mere photographic defect, as a confirmation of this baseless fancy. Foolishness of this kind has nothing to support it in science or religion; it is an offence against both. We have no reason to regard the Pleiades as the centre of the universe, or as containing the attracting mass which draws our sun forward in its vast mysterious orbit.

R. H. Allen, in his survey of the literature of the Pleiades, mentions that "Drach surmised that their midnight culmination in the time of Moses, ten days after the autumnal equinox, may have fixed the Day of Atonement on the 10th of Tishri."[221:1] This is worth quoting as a sample of the unhappy astronomical guesses of commentators. Drach overlooked that his suggestion necessitated the assumption that in the time of Moses astronomers had already learned, first, to determine the actual equinox; next, to observe the culmination of stars on the meridian rather than their risings and settings; and, third and more important, to determine midnight by some artificial measurement of time. None of these can have been primitive operations; we have no knowledge that any of the three were in use in the time of Moses; certainly they were not suitable for a people on the march, like the Israelites in the wilderness. Above all, Drach ignored in this suggestion the fact that the Jewish calendar was a lunar-solar one, and hence that the tenth day of the seventh month could not bear any fixed relation either to the autumnal equinox, or to the midnight culmination of the Pleiades; any more than our Easter Sunday is fixed to the spring equinox on March 22.

The Pleiades were often associated with the late autumn, as Aratus writes—

> "Men mark them rising with Sol's setting light,
> Forerunners of the winter's gloomy night."

This is what is technically known as the "acronical rising" of the Pleiades, their rising at sunset; in contrast to their "heliacal rising," their rising just before daybreak, which ushered in the spring time. This acronical rising has led to the association of the group with the rainy season, and with floods. Thus Statius called the cluster "Pliadum nivosum sidus," and Valerius Flaccus distinctly used the word "Pliada" for the showers. Josephus says that during the siege of Jerusalem by Antiochus Epiphanes in 170 b.c., the besieged wanted for water until relieved "by a large shower of rain which fell at the setting of the Pleiades." R. H. Allen, in his *Star-Names and their Meanings*, states that the Pleiades "are intimately connected with traditions of the flood found among so many and widely separated nations, and especially in the Deluge-myth of Chaldæa," but he does not cite authorities or instances.

The Talmud gives a curious legend connecting the Pleiades with the Flood:—

> "When the Holy One, blessed be He! wished to bring the Deluge upon the world, He took two stars out of Pleiades, and thus let the Deluge loose. And when He wished to arrest it, He took two stars out of Arcturus and stopped it."[223:1]

It would seem from this that the Rabbis connected the number of visible stars with the number of the family in the Ark—with the "few, that is, eight souls . . . saved by water," of whom St. Peter speaks. Six Pleiades only are usually seen by the naked eye; traditionally seven were seen; but the Rabbis assumed that two, not one, were lost.

Perhaps we may trace a reference to this supposed association of *Kīmah* with the Flood in the passage from Amos already quoted:—

> "Seek Him that maketh the seven stars and Orion, . . . that calleth for the waters of the sea, and poureth them out upon the face of the earth: the Lord is His name."

Many ancient nations have set apart days in the late autumn in honour of the dead, no doubt because the year was then considered as dead. This season being marked by the acronical rising of the Pleiades, that group has become associated with such observances. There is, however, no reference to any custom of this kind in Scripture.

What is the meaning of the inquiry addressed to Job by the Almighty?

"Canst thou bind the sweet influences of Pleiades?"

What was the meaning which it possessed in the thought of the writer of the book? What was the meaning which we should now put on such an inquiry, looking at the constellations from the standpoint which the researches of modern astronomy have given us?

The first meaning of the text would appear to be connected with the apparent movement of the sun amongst the stars in the course of the year. We cannot see the stars by daylight, or see directly where the sun is situated with respect to them; but, in very early times, men learnt to associate the seasons of the year with the stars which were last seen in the morning, above the place where the sun was about to rise; in the technical term once in use, with the heliacal risings of stars. When the constellations were first designed, the Pleiades rose heliacally at the beginning of April, and were the sign of the return of spring. Thus Aratus, in his constellation poem writes—

"Men mark them (*i. e.* the Pleiades) rising with the solar ray,
   The harbinger of summer's brighter day."

They heralded, therefore, the revival of nature from her winter sleep, the time of which the kingly poet sang so alluringly—

"For, lo, the winter is past,
   The rain is over and gone;
The flowers appear on the earth;
   The time of the singing of birds is come,
And the voice of the turtle is heard in our land;
   The fig-tree ripeneth her green figs,
And the vines are in blossom,
   They give forth their fragrance."

The constellation which thus heralded the return of this genial season was poetically taken as representing the power and influence of spring. Their "sweet influences" were those that had rolled away the gravestone of snow and ice which had lain upon the winter tomb of nature. Theirs was the power that brought the flowers up from under the turf; earth's constellations of a million varied stars to shine upwards in answer to the constellations of heaven above. Their influences filled copse and wood with the songs of happy birds. Theirs stirred anew the sap in the veins of the trees, and drew forth their reawakened strength in bud and blossom. Theirs was the bleating of the new-born lambs; theirs the murmur of the reviving bees.

Upon this view, then, the question to Job was, in effect, "What control hast thou over the powers of nature? Canst thou hold back the sun from shining in spring-time—from quickening flower, and herb, and tree with its gracious warmth? This is God's work, year by year over a thousand lands, on a million hills, in a million valleys. What canst thou do to hinder it?"

The question was a striking one; one which must have appealed to the patriarch, evidently a keen observer and lover of nature; and it was entirely in line with the other inquiries addressed to him in the same chapter.

"Where wast thou when I laid the foundations of the earth?"

The Revised Version renders the question—

"Canst thou bind the *cluster* of the Pleiades?"

reading the Hebrew word *Ma'anaddoth*, instead of *Ma'adannoth*, following in this all the most ancient versions. On this view, Job is, in effect, asked, "Canst thou gather together the stars in the family of the Pleiades and keep them in their places?"

The expression of a chain or band is one suggested by the appearance of the group to the eye, but it is no less appropriate in the knowledge which photography and great telescopes have given us. To quote from Miss Clerke's description of the nebula discovered round the brighter stars of the Pleiades—Alcyone, Asterope, Celœno, Electra, Maia, Merope and Taygeta:—

> "Besides the Maia vortex, the Paris photographs depicted a series of nebulous bars on either side of Merope, and a curious streak extending like a finger-post from Electra towards Alcyone . . . Streamers and fleecy masses of cosmical fog seem almost to fill the spaces between the stars, as clouds choke a mountain valley. The chief points of its concentration are the four stars Alcyone, Merope, Maia, and Electra; but it includes as well Celœno and Taygeta, and is traceable southward from Asterope over an arc of 1° 10´. . . . The greater part of the constellation is shown as veiled in nebulous matter of most unequal densities. In some places it lies in heavy folds and wreaths, in others it barely qualifies the darkness of the sky-ground. The details of its distribution come out with remarkable clearness, and are evidently to a large extent prescribed by the relative situations of the stars. Their lines of junction are frequently marked by nebulous rays, establishing between them, no doubt, re-

lations of great physical importance; and masses of nebula, in numerous instances, seem as if *pulled out of shape* and drawn into festoons by the attractions of neighbouring stars. But the strangest exemplification of this filamentous tendency is in a fine, thread-like process, 3´´ or 4´´ wide, but 35´ to 40´ long, issuing in an easterly direction from the edge of the nebula about Maia, and stringing together seven stars, met in its advance, like beads on a rosary. The largest of these is apparently the occasion of a slight deviation from its otherwise rectilinear course. A second similar but shorter streak runs, likewise east and west, through the midst of the formation."[229:1]

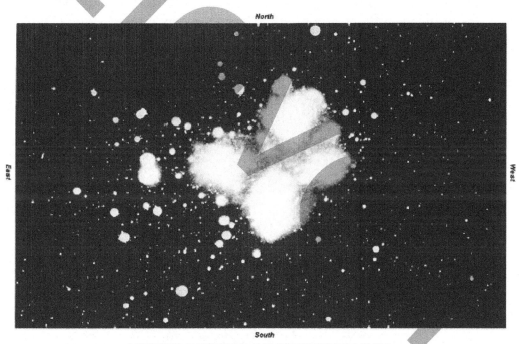

NEBULOSITIES OF THE PLEIADES.
Photographed by Dr. Max Wolf, Heidelberg.ToList

Later photographs have shown that not only are the several stars of the Pleiades linked together by nebulous filaments, but the whole cluster is embedded in a nebulous net that spreads its meshes far out into space. Not only is the group thus tied or bound together by nebulous clouds, it has other tokens of forming but a single family. The movements of the several stars have been carefully measured, and for the most part the entire cluster is drifting in the same direction; a few stars do not share in the common motion, and are probably apparent members, seen in perspective projected on the group, but in reality much nearer to us. The members of the group also show a family likeness in constitution. When the spectroscope is turned upon it, the chief stars are seen to closely resemble each other;

the principal lines in their spectra being those of hydrogen, and these are seen as broad and diffused bands, so that the spectrum we see resembles that of the brightest star of the heavens, Sirius.

There can be little doubt but that the leaders of the group are actually greater, brighter suns than Sirius itself. We do not know the exact distance of the Pleiades, they are so far off that we can scarcely do more than make a guess at it; but it is probable that they are so far distant that our sun at like distance would prove much too faint to be seen at all by the naked eye. The Pleiades then would seem to be a most glorious star-system, not yet come to its full growth. From the standpoint of modern science we may interpret the "chain" or "the sweet influences" of the Pleiades as consisting in the enfolding wisps of nebulosity which still, as it were, knit together those vast young suns; or, and in all probability more truly, as that mysterious force of gravitation which holds the mighty system together, and in obedience to which the group has taken its present shape. The question, if asked us to-day, would be, in effect, "Canst thou bind together by nebulous chains scores of suns, far more glorious than thine own, and scattered over many millions of millions of miles of space; or canst thou loosen the attraction which those suns exercise upon each other, and move them hither and thither at thy will?"

FOOTNOTES:

[217:1] *Glossary of Greek Birds*, pp. 28, 29.

[221:1] R. H. Allen, *Star Names and their Meanings*, p. 401.

[223:1] *Berachoth*, fol. 59, col. 1.

[229:1] *The System of the Stars*, 1st edit., pp. 230-232.

Week 15 Activity

Astronomy Club Report

Make contact with an Astronomy Club in your area; then go visit one of their evening star gazing events. Write a one page paper describing your experience. Who did you find? How did you find them? Where did you go? When did you go? What did you see and learn that evening?   How did you like the experience?   The paper is due any time before the last week of class.

Made in the USA
Monee, IL
11 June 2023

35624499R00057